A Tormented mind

Childhood Trauma in Adulthood

ROCKY TROIANI

MAPLE
PUBLISHERS

My Tormented Mind

Author: Rocky Troiani

Copyright © Rocky Troiani (2022)

The right of Rocky Troiani to be identified as author of this work has been asserted by the author in accordance with section 77 and 78 of the Copyright, Designs and Patents Act 1988.

First Published in 2022

ISBN 978-1-915492-56-2 (Paperback)
      978-1-915492-57-9 (E-Book)

Book cover design and Book layout by:
      White Magic Studios
      www.whitemagicstudios.co.uk

Published by:
      Maple Publishers
      1 Brunel Way,
      Slough,
      SL1 1FQ, UK
      www.maplepublishers.com

CONTENTS

Chapter 1 – The Baby Steps into Life.............................6

Chapter 2 – My Journey into Adulthood 11

Chapter 3 – Desperate Measures................................18

Chapter 4 – My Trusting Heart 24

Chapter 5 – The Tears of a Heart Broken Mother............36

Chapter 6 – The Echoes of the Prison Walls..................50

Chapter 7 – The Discovery of Me 61

Chapter 8 – Freedom to an Uncertain Path...................71

Chapter 9 – I'm Just a Soul whose Intentions are Good.....83

Chapter 10 – Discovering your Purpose in Life................99

Chapter 11 – You have my Heart in your Hands 110

Chapter 12 – Let me bring you Every Kind Smiles...........121

Chapter 13 – Pride of Britain...................................130

Chapter 14 – Sons are the Anchors of a Mother's Life 145

Chapter 15 – The Devil came for me Again 156

Chapter 16 – Laying your Demons to Rest....................169

The Final Word...182

Acknowledgments..195

Preface (Introduction)

From the moment we are born into this life, the very moment we take our first breath and the very second the umbilical cord is cut, life, as we know it, is down to us. Our parents aid our path as guides to our journey in life. As the duty of any good parent they guide us with the hope we succeed. We may have brothers or sisters with us as we grow into this world and live to love one another and bond as a family. As children, our minds are computers taking in a wealth of information, good and bad, which moulds our character into the person we learn to become. During the seventies mental health was not in the forefront, hardly talked about or recognised. From children to adults we just got on with things, whatever the consequences which could lead to catastrophic results as you will read within this book. The results of this almost brought my world to an end.

Your childhood plays a massive part in your forthcoming years. It determines your outcome in many ways. Your childhood computes your path. This can stem from your parents, your brothers, your sisters, your cousins, your uncles, your aunts, your family and schooling. They are the teachers who feed your path in later life. Child mental health can sometimes go unseen from spending too much time alone subjected to raging temper tantrums, bullying from all angles from school to family members. For the children of today's world, it's worse than ever, to the point of suicides at a young age. This is the true story of a journey from my childhood right up to my later years. I cannot push forward enough that this story may just help another person that may have suffered child abuse. Mental health is a very large subject in today's society, however, I've lived to tell the tale. I will share my experiences, share my tears and fears, share my smiles and laughter knowing deep down in my heart and soul, that despite being convinced I was a bad person from childhood, I managed to reinvent myself and re-programme my mind to who I really, deeply am, later in life. When we are born none of us are born horrible or nasty; it's our surroundings and the people around us that dictate our character. We are the seed of life, the creation of a journey ahead, one that's filled with experiences from every emotion from sadness to happiness, to live, love and laugh, and to fulfil a life with a purpose which can be destroyed by those we love, too. Many years ago, I wrote my then life story on paper whilst serving seven years for conspiracy to commit armed robbery on a drug dealing nightclub in Kent. For three years I wrote an autobiography. This autobiography was my therapy. It was my escape from my concrete room with my AM FM radio, my small table, my windows that only opened an inch or two to the stale smell of a concrete room which was mopped with a stale mop. The echoes of the convicts, the keys rattling, jingle, jingle, along with the slop out pot under the bed. I had time to think. So, it was pen to paper. For three years I put my feelings down on paper, how I felt inside as a person, as a friend, as a son, as a human. Was I this person I was made out to be? Was I the person that I was told I was? Prison gave me discovery.

The autobiography was never published, it wasn't the right time. I hadn't lived the life that was coming, it had only just started, the journey had just begun. We all will go through life and live experiences, good and bad. It moulds who we are. Life had certainly tested me to the limits of contemplating suicide. Years of torture of being told how horrible I was by a family member. In the end I was convinced I was that person. This short introduction is just an insight into my journey of life which is why I would hope this book gives an insight into 'Hope', and that there's light at the end of that dark cold tunnel and gives emphasis into how important a child's upbringing really is. I'm going to share with you my experiences of The Good, the Bad and the Ugly. Follow my journey within this book and the outcome which potentially has saved my life and the beautiful people that never left my side. Learning to talk and open up deep, dark emotions that need addressing is truly essential for healing the soul and moving on in life.

Finding a spiritual ground and using nature and faith as your guide whilst taking in the beauty of life which is there; we just have to stop, look and listen. I found counselling (Life coaching) a valuable true path which has helped me open my heart and learn to talk about my darkness and learn to live again. As I now reach the 52nd year of my life, I finally find myself and fill the blank pages of my journey that was destined to be my purpose. Now I live my life to bring hope and help others to smile in the darkest times of their lives. Never give up.

Chapter 1

The Baby Steps into Life

The baby steps of life, the beginning of everything in life. I was born in a very small, terraced house, a two-up two-down property, small and cramped, but home. My father worked as an iron caulker in Chatham Naval Dockyard. Generations of our family worked in the Naval Dockyard. My father's surname was 'Sands' which I inherited.

Life during the 70s was fun. People cared about one another. Your neighbour would bring a dinner around for you and people smiled and people laughed. There was no internet, there was no Facebook, no Instagram, no pretending to be something you weren't, no mobile phones; very rarely heard of suicide and very rarely heard of mental health issues. Life during the 70s was beautiful, lots of pubs through Chatham, full of happy people. Smoking was allowed in pubs, bat and ball in the garden, and you could go and play outside without the fear that we have today. I loved the 70s flared trousers, Marc Bolan platform shoes and real music. In my opinion, my generation had the best decades within the 50s, 60s and specially for me the 70s and 80s. Life was real. Growing up in the 70s was great. I would love to turn the clock back and live those decades again, the reason being because they were the most secure and easy times of my life, thanks to my lovely mother and father.

My father used to talk about the days of Sugarloaf Hill in Chatham which was a Romany gypsy site. Chatham had its fair share of Romany gipsies, good people, kind people and some very hard people, too. My mother was originally from Italy and came to England in 1952 and lived with her sister. I loved the Italian way. I loved the food, the strength of a family bond, the unity, and most of all, the love from family members.

I loved my nana. She was amazing. She used to sit with me when I needed to sing songs, and smiled at me and loved me. It was beautiful. My mother had two sisters and one brother. One sister and brother lived in Italy, which we visited during the 70s.

My mother had a daughter from a previous marriage, in which her husband was an aggressive alcoholic, and violent. She was brought up with this image and this way of life during my mother's first marriage. My sister was almost ten years older than me, my sister was present when I was born in Luton Road, Chatham. As the years went on up to around seven years old life was so beautiful. I have images of memories that will never leave me. Specifically, as the years went on, unbeknown to me, my mental state of mind was developing and also, unbeknown to me, I was developing mental health issues that I never even knew of, at that time.

I was approximately seven or eight years old when I discovered I was hated by my sister. The resentment was extremely strong. The resentment was anger and jealousy. Every negative emotion that you could possibly think of, was present within my sister. During those years, specifically, around seven and eight years, something happened to me that has never left me and would stay with me throughout my adult years to the present. I will refer to the name of this person as 'Miss Evil'. I was taken to a bedroom with her friend where the door was locked behind me. I could see that face that she used to have when she was going to bully and intimidate me. It gave me that worthless feeling. To tell me I was a horrible little boy and nasty little boy, spoilt little brat, intimidated more and more and more. But on this particular day whilst being locked in a bedroom with herself and her friend, the bedroom shared with two single beds, on either side of the room. 'Miss Evil' got in her bed and her friend got in the other and I was made to get in bed with her friend.

I can remember turning around not sure what was going on, not sure about what was about to happen, but smiling as I thought we were playing. This person and her friend were approximately ten years older than me which made them around eighteen years old, they were no children. The sneering face is still vivid in my thoughts, the sneering face of anger and intimidation and bullying, and telling me to take her friend's clothes off. At this point I still thought we were playing. I was a child, I was a baby, I knew nothing of the wrongdoing of what was happening at this point. Sexual assault took place, of which the rest of the assault was a blur to me.

I can remember being told to take the girl's bra off and looking around at this person with her aggressive face taunting me, go on, go on. Whilst this assault was taking place. my mother was banging on the bedroom door, shouting, "Let me in, let me in. What's going on what's going on?" Unbeknown to my mother a sexual assault was taking place. She knew something wasn't right, she could not enter the bedroom because this family member had locked the door. The rest is history, and the rest of this history affected me for the rest of my life. Flashbacks to that day are still very apparent. Images of the aggressive face of 'Miss Evil' have never left me and to this day still live with me which changed the rest of my life and took away all the trust, all the belief, all the faith I had in any woman. How could someone that you love so much want to destroy you so badly?

That aggressive sneering face was a continuation of bullying, intimidation, fuelled with alcohol and drugs that this family member continuously gave me. I can recall many occasions where she would set out to turn the rest of the family against me - my cousins, my aunts, my uncles, my mother and my father; her goal was to destroy me and destroy my soul, take my sanity, steal my trust, and kill my belief in anyone that I loved.

As a child your mind is a computer. The most intricate part of anything in this life is your mind. Once you have seen something, once something has happened to you that never leaves you, good or bad, and traumatic events will always stay with you. As a child, any child, whatever happens to you will reflect in your later years as a person, as a character, as a human being. Your childhood events will reflect in your later years. These events that took place in my childhood reflected in everything I did which made me aggressive at the age of seven and eight years old. Ten years old and onwards I used to lose my temper, punch doors, punch walls, kick things, smash things up. The aggression was immense.

This unnatural character of mine was developed as a result of being bullied, intimidated and sexually assaulted, instigated by a family member. How could this be done to me when all I wanted to do was love? As I reached my teens the aggression got worse. My mother and father were afraid of me, terrified of even saying the wrong thing, but deep down I was a caring soul, I just wanted to be loved. My sister left home at eighteen years old for some crazy reason. I actually missed her. She was my half-sister from my mother's first marriage but she was my sister despite what she did to me. At my age of seven years my parents purchased a dog from our local pet shop. I can remember the day as if it was yesterday, when I chose this little black bundle of fluff. I named her Blackie. She became my soulmate and my world of unconditional love which I learned from an early age was beautiful, kind and unconditional. When I reached fourteen years I started boxing. I loved it and had a couple of fights. It taught me discipline and respect, but boxing was not destined for me; weightlifting was. I was inspired from a young age by the Rocky films. I love them. The Rocky films were so inspirational. I loved the way Rocky was portrayed, coming from the deep, within the dark streets of no hope, to becoming a champion; so inspirational.

I bought myself some weights from Argos, just some simple plastic weights and a barbell. I wanted to feel strong as a person. I wanted to feel Powerful. I wanted to feel in control of my life. I needed to be somebody. I wanted to be loved, even as a visual look as a bodybuilder, weightlifter, whatever you want to call it. After years of being made to feel worthless, small and insignificant, I needed to feel strong in heart and soul, and weight training was the start for me. But with weightlifting, knowledge began to grow and with that, the introduction of steroids.

Bearing in mind the aggression that was built in me, the steroids fuelled the fire within. The anger within me, within my heart and soul from childhood, was bad. For years I've been bullied by a family member. Intimidation made me feel worthless, small and unimportant.

That was how I felt inside and this was about to come out in a bad way. This is where the story really begins.

Chapter 2

My Journey into Adulthood

My late teens were a great time in my life, especially when I passed my driving test at seventeen years. I was blessed with a father that bought me my first car. It was a Ford Escort Mark one in Sahara beige and I loved this car. It was only £250 but it meant the world to me for my first taste of freedom as a man, or nearly a man, and I loved it. When you're young you feel indestructible. Nothing can hurt you, nothing can come near you, you fear nothing ahead of you and you think life is forever. You think life is eternal that it's never going to end and that the people that you have around you and the ones that you love are also there eternally and there is no end to life. After my teenage years, I stormed into my twenties', hormones raging, fuelled with steroids, training daily, pumping the blood with sports enhancing drugs; getting bigger and stronger, and life was exciting.

You don't realise when you're in your twenties' that life could change any second. Like I said, it's eternal, it's forever, nothing is going to end, but one thing is sure for me - my past, my childhood was going to play a big part in the journey ahead in my life. Everything that was inside me, unbeknown to me at one point in my life, was going to come to a boiling point. And another thing that was for sure - at that particular moment in time nothing mattered, nothing at all. I used to love driving around, listening to my tape deck in my car, mainly the group White snake, loved the tune, 'In the Still of the Night' blaring out loud with my Harvard speakers placed neatly on my rear parcel shelf of the car.

Life could not have been better. My mother, my father, my family were all present and beautiful. For a little while I worked for a company called Bradley and Reeds who were running a fine limit sheet metal workshop in Chatham. My time there was limited due to a heated argument with a workmate. I was only seventeen. This was something my sister had said which fuelled this argument. The man I had an argument with was probably fifteen years older than me, a grown man. I was just a teenager. He grabbed me by the collar on my overalls and threatened me, so I grabbed him by the collar of his overalls and shoved him back whilst picking up a Stanley knife, and swiftly sweeping it across his chest, thankfully missing him as he stepped back.

This was my first encounter with a man and my first encounter of who I was and what I had become. I quickly realised there was something else inside me. Violence was no problem, where had that little innocent little boy gone, where had he gone and where did this animal come from? I realised there was no in-between with my temper, there was no discussion when that Instinct within me was born, the programming of my childhood from being bullied, intimidated, made to feel insignificant, made to feel small, that screwed up face I saw in that man was the face of this family member; the taunting, the aggression in the eyes, the anger was all very apparent within a split second. But this time I could hit out, I could deal with it, violence with violence. I was removed from the company. The police were not involved and my parents never found out what had become of me and where was it going to take me.

Girlfriends slowly came into my life. The interest in sex was strong. I had no interest in having children. I was far too young, too much to live for, too much to experience. To be held down by children - it wasn't what I wanted but it happened to a girl I was seeing. She fell pregnant and before I knew it, I was a father. The relationship was destined to fail. We had nothing in common at all but it was my stupidity of not taking precautions that caused a pregnancy and I felt it was my duty that I should see things through, bearing in mind I was only twenty-one years old, still a child and she was just eighteen; we were kids.

She already had a child of her own which was from a previous relationship, that was already two years old, but I thought it was the right thing to do to stand by her. My mother and my father were looking at finding a flat, a ground floor flat as my dad's health had deteriorated. We realised he had heart disease and lung problems. It probably was a result of working in Chatham Dockyard for almost fifty years. There was no protective clothing back then, there were no respirators, there was no Health and Safety. After fifty years of working in Chatham Dockyard his health took a decline so a ground floor flat was required. At this time, we were still living in the house I was born in, along Luton Road in Chatham. My mother and my father found a flat which they proceeded to move into and let myself and my then girlfriend and children live within the house and for me to take over the tenancy of the house I was born in.

I struggled with life's commitment to be a family man but it was my duty and I could not walk away from my daughter that had been born. I found a job as a labourer on a building site and hated every second of it. I would argue regularly with other workers due to that feeling once again as if I was as a kid to be pushed around and intimidated; something I didn't take too lightly.

Things were about to take a turn for the worst. My father one day was sitting in the flat they had just moved into with my mother, and my year-old daughter was on his knee. As I walked into the room I saw my father smiling happily, my mother laughing happily, my daughter just smiling, happy sitting on my father's knee, but I had no interest in this. I had a car that needed fixing which was outside the flat and I needed a pipe for it, so I asked my father, "Would you go to the shop for me, Dad, and pick up this pipe for the car so I can start driving again as I've got no car?" His reply was, "What for, bloody cars!" He reluctantly placed my daughter down onto the floor to play with her toys, reluctantly stood up, reluctantly went to grab his coat and reluctantly walked outside with me where I could show him the part that I needed for the car.

I walked my father to the car and explained to him, "Dad that's the bit I need. Nev Andrews motor store is open. If you wouldn't mind getting it for me that would be great," as he looked up at me in disgust and said to me, "What do you think I am – batchy?" These were the very last words he said to me as I saw him walking down the alley with his raincoat on; the last vision I had of my Father, the very last words that were said to me and the very last image I had of him walking down the alley to obtain a part for a car for me which I could have walked down to pick up but I didn't. I asked a sixty-nine- year old man to go to the shop for me which was his last walk ever.

Hours had passed; at that point I never knew my father had died. The call came from Medway Hospital. I never knew he never made it to the shop but the call was one I will never forget. I dropped my daughter off. I took my mother to the hospital to see my father where we were asked to come into a small room and then told that my father had passed away and was dead on arrival at Medway Hospital. This was my very first taste of losing someone so beautiful, someone so special, someone so unique, someone I didn't appreciate as much as I should have done; someone I wish I had shown more love to and someone I wished I had appreciated more, but it was all too late. The man that loved me, the man that dedicated his life to put food on the table for me, the man that showed me love in his own way; we never cuddled, we never embraced as father and son. This was a man of a generation that was totally different to ours; this was a man of a generation that would wear a shirt and tie every day or a blazer, always would wear shoes never trainers, that generation we will never see again. He always shaved, was always smart, a man of dignity, a man of truth and a man that stood no nonsense. I watched my mother lean over my dead father crying so deeply, crying for the love of her life that was gone forever. It was me that had asked him to go to the shop for me while I was too lazy and too ignorant to go there myself. I felt like I had caused my father's death. My mother kept shouting, "My Ron my Ron." I stood behind my mother in shock, looking at my father with his raincoat on and his shoes, with his eyes closed, his face white grey with his mouth slightly open and my mum leaning on his chest in tears, crying, and I believed I was the cause of this. That vision will never leave me. It will haunt me until my dying day, but I didn't know how much this had affected me. I didn't realise what was ahead of me and certainly, I didn't realise what had become of me.

From that day on, from that moment on, my life was about to change paths, was going to change the journey ahead, was definitely going to change. The other part of me was going to become real, the dark part, the part I never actually knew was there, was going to be very apparent. The journey ahead was certainly one I could never have predicted and certainly one that was going to change my life forever.

My father's funeral was arranged. The vision of my mother standing by my father's grave as I held her in my arms was painful beyond words. I never knew the severity of the damage that had been done but I could witness my father being lowered into a hole. I was twenty-three years old. My relationship had failed with my daughter's mother. I was told that there was a strong possibility that my daughter was not mine. This was a further hurtful smash to my already beaten soul from women. My experiences were showing me even more, so I just could not trust any women as these are people that profess to love me - how can anyone be so hurtful and unkind? I never believed anything that they told me or had faith in any woman at all and believed my daughter was not mine- as why would anyone say this if it was not true? With all this in mind, I wanted to be on my own. Within the coffin of my father I laid a photo of what my father believed was his granddaughter, who was the very last person he held in his arms, was that little girl whom he treasured. Also, a photo of me and my mother within his coffin that my father could take to heaven with him. I left a little note with him to say, "look over us and protect us and to protect his devoted wife, my beautiful mother."

After the funeral myself, my mother and my sister returned home. My father had a son from a previous marriage, many years older than me. His name was Ken. Ken had offered £100 to my mother to help towards the funeral, a funeral that my mother could not afford to pay for as we discovered there was no funeral plan, there was no life insurance, there was no policy, there was nothing. We were broke, flat broke, not a penny left, not a penny to our name, completely broke. I thought the £100 as an insult and to this day I still say it was an insult as even in 1993 the funeral cost almost three and a half thousand pounds which we didn't have. I didn't make a fuss, I didn't kick off but I thought it was disrespectful to offer £100. As it was his father he should have at least paid half.

This was when I discovered something I had suspicions of discovering; that my sister hated me. This was my first taste of hate from her. I was not a young boy anymore. I was not a child. I was a twenty-three years old man that understood hate, understood that screwed up face that looked over me, that screwed up face of evil as she snared towards me pointing a finger and with these words that never left me, "I have never loved you as a brother." These were drug filled drunken words spoken, of truth, of what she really thought of me. Realisation kicked in, my questions were answered, my doubts resolved. My sister hated me with a passion. The flashbacks to my childhood, taunted, bullied intimidated, hated, all came out. Within those words, confirmation was achieved. My sister was in agreement with my dad's son regarding the hundred pounds as sufficient towards the funeral costs. This was not my sister defending my mother which she should have been. This was her opportunity to take my soul, that snaring face of evil. We were broke, we had no money, we had nothing left. My sister defended my step brother and not me or her mother but this was her way of finishing me off.

That very day they buried two people. They buried my father and they buried my sister as those words would never leave me, 'I have never loved you as a brother'. This was the sister that I loved despite what she had done to me, the sister that I cared for despite the bullying for years. She had done that to me, broken my heart, stamped on my soul and kicked me while I was down. How could anyone do that to their brother on the day they buried their father? How could any human do that when they claim to love you, claim to care for you? But this was the confirmation I needed as deep within my heart and soul I knew something wasn't right for many years but I needed confirmation to clear my doubts.

The next part of this journey was about to change my life forever, as for many years my sister put my aggression down to steroids. All she ever said to my mother for many, many years - it's the steroids, he's aggressive because of the steroids. At that time after years of being told I was a horrible person, after years of being tortured, 'you are a nasty human being', I believed it. I accepted that it must be who I am. I must be the horrible person that my sister says I am, despite the confirmation of telling me she never loved me as a brother on the day they buried my father. Part of me was telling me, maybe some of the stuff that she been had telling me is true, maybe I deserved what I got, the punishment that I got. After all, I did ask my father to go to the shop for me to pick up a part for the car. I must be that horrible person, that steroid fuelled aggressive twenty-three years old man.

Things were about to go onto the next level in life for me, another level I would never have expected or anticipated; as Clive Sands was this horrible person and I was about to get more horrible. The things that my sister had done to me as a child must have been justified, must have been my fault. It must have been my fault when my sister instigated her friend to sexually assault me. I blamed myself, it must have been my fault.

So now I was going to be that person I was told I was. I was like a wild caged lion; aggressive, hated life, suffered no fools. The chapter of my life was going to be one that would probably break me but I was willing to take all the risks as when I walked away from my dying father that lay on that hospital bed, I promised him I would take care of his devoted wife, my mother, for him, no matter what. And one thing in this life - I never break a promise that I give and I would hold that promise whatever it took. I was going to take care of my mother, no matter what the cost.

⚫━◆⟨▶⟩◆━⚫

Chapter 3

Desperate Measures

The journey ahead was going to be one I would never forget. Prison never scared me, never bothered me. In my opinion at the time I had nothing to lose, but I did have everything to lose and that was my mother, all 4-ft 8 of her typical little Italian, bubbly, smiling, always happy, jolly, loving to help people, loving to help the elderly ones of life's angels. A genuine, beautiful, loving, kind soul, she was an example of life. I loved my mother. She was my life, she was my everything, she was my world, she was my entirety and my soul.

One particular day, on coming back from the gym I discovered my little soulmate, Blackie, lying there on the floor, her tongue pushed to one side. I could not see her breathing. She wasn't moving. I leant over Blackie. I looked at her and to my horror and shock I realised that she had died. This for me was a devastating blow to a soul that gave me nothing but unconditional love, pure unconditional love. Love without a motive is the most beautifulest gift in the world and that little dog gave me that for many, many years and that was gone forever.

I buried my dog in my garden, my beautiful soulmate, I kissed her goodbye. I hoped within my heart that someday we would meet again and she would be my first vision when I entered heaven. Life couldn't get any worse for me. I was struggling mentally more than I realised. I would be driving my car and suddenly burst into tears, I would pull over and cry. Half the time I would not know what I was crying for - was it my past, was it my childhood, was it the loss of my father, the loss of my dog, the loss of a daughter I thought I had? Was I losing my sanity? I was so unsure of what was going on with me but one thing I did know; I kept crying and I just did not understand why. I thought I had dealt with everything within me. Clearly, I hadn't.

I had so much anger inside me, so much aggression and there was no way it was being released. Where does aggression go when it's not released? It goes deep. What is anger? Is it a punishment we give ourselves due to someone else's doing that makes us so aggressive?

I had a promise to keep to my father so I set out to find employment, try and find a job, a normal everyday job to help my mother pay for a funeral she could not afford. We were broke, we had no money, and due to the argument I had had with my sister she did not bother contacting us at all. That relationship between me and my sister had come to an end.

Finding employment was impossible. I had no qualifications, I was expelled from school at 15. The last job that I had, I almost stabbed someone. I knew, for me, working for someone was an impossibility. During my training days I became close friends with a great guy called Steve Tannahill. My dad loved him, Steve was about ten years older than me; one of life's good people. We did a little bit of buying and selling of cars which kept us ticking over but I had other ideas; ideas that would probably bring us good money and this led me into car ringing, the changing of number plates and tags and even doubling up cars. I used to pay local car thieves to steal cars for me to order and I would change the identity and sell them.

This became very fruitful and was beginning to earn us money. I thought I would have a go at stealing cars. Me and Steve would set out to find the car we needed. However, one particular day whilst looking for a car in the local car park two police cars stopped us, searched the car and found a scaffold tube and screwdriver. Obviously, these were sure signs of what they called "going equipped." This put a screaming halt to our car ringing racket. Myself and Steve were charged with going equipped. With further searches to our properties they found vehicle number plates and tags. We both ended up in court and had 180 hours community service orders for us. This was the end of our car ringing days but not my determination to make more money. I was fuelled by aggression and the promise I had given to my father.

I thought the world of Steve, we were like brothers, he was like the brother I never had - a powerfully built man that loved powerlifting. He was extremely fit and could run miles. A man of endurance and power – I absolutely loved him. My dear mother was struggling to pay for the funeral. She took up a little part-time job washing dishes in a cafe, my dear mother had no choice. With this in mind I popped into a local nightclub in Gillingham to ask if they needed any nightclub security. I have never done this before but needs must. The nightclub was called Excalibur nightclub, a massive nightclub run by a Maltese family. I just wanted to work at the club door and earn some money.

These were the days of black suits, white shirts and bow tie. There were no rules; we are talking about the days of nightclub bouncers. If you play up, you would get a clump that's it. I can live with that but I'd never been tested and this was my opportunity to be tested. I started work the following weekend.

As the weeks and days and months went on I worked the nightclub doors every weekend. Violence became a second nature. It didn't bother me how big they were, what their reputation was, I just wasn't bothered. The gym and steroids were a big part of my life and so was aggression. I feared nothing, but if you met me I would show you respect. I would shake your hand, be polite, be courteous and I would be kind. That was my nature but deep within me there was a demon. He wasn't nice and I didn't like him.

Where was this life taking me? What was my purpose to be on this planet as I went through the 90s? Life was getting worse, money was a problem, my mother was struggling, I was struggling, my mind was struggling. I was still having moments when I would just cry. I had no reason; it felt at the time I would just cry.

I had left Excalibur nightclub and started work on nightclub doors in Maidstone. I began to get a little bit of a reputation, which I never knew I had. I was slightly muscular and hit the gym really hard. I had to be strong, I had to feel big, I had to be powerful. I did a lot of bag work in the gym, and pad work. I was not a hard man. I didn't see myself as a hard man. I saw myself as a reasonable man that didn't suffer fools gladly.

I remember reading a book by Geoff Thompson. I found it a very interesting book about a nightclub doorman and his experiences working on nightclub doors. In one paragraph in that book it told of a situation where he was outnumbered and how he would deal with that outnumbered situation by losing it badly – shouting, raging, foaming at the mouth, ready to kill. That paragraph never left me and when I entered situations where I thought I was outnumbered I would use that method and used it many, many times after and it worked every time. I would portray a raging psychopath. People would think, 'leave that well alone, he's a nutter'. I worked with a guy called Matt Ploughman, a big 6-ft 4 rugby player. I loved the guy. He just didn't care, feared nothing and we clicked right away. I worked at a nightclub called Zoots, and Matt Ploughman wanted me to take the door over and I did. During the 90s there was no need for doormen to have security badges. However, these came in 1995. The old school doorman used old methods and took people out the back exit and gave them a pasting; that was the old ways - that's how people learnt respect, that's how the job was done.

I would have glass collectors within the club selling drugs for me. It was my extra bit of money and a new line for me. I became addicted to Speed. I spent many days trying to recover from the drug and the comedown was nasty; days of paranoia were horrendous. But It was my escape from reality, it was my escape from everything. Steve Tannahill and I were very close and decided to work at another nightclub due to a fight at Zoots nightclub which I was involved in. I had to leave. In fact, I was ordered to leave and I started work at the Union Bar, Maidstone.

We were still a struggling family. The money I was earning was only paying bills. Life was not great and it was about to take a turn for the worst. I was selling drugs, mainly Ecstasy and Speed. It was my little income. I would supply, mainly, doormen and they then sold it throughout their clubs. It's how it was done during the 90s. Ecstasy was the big seller, it was the main drug of the day. Especially during the mid 90s, Ecstasy was the drug.

I didn't enjoy selling drugs. It wasn't my path but it was a little extra money at the time. I still had no direction in my life. I couldn't hold a full-time job down. I struggled tolerating people. In fact, I didn't like people. Every relationship I entered into was a disaster, a pure disaster. I trusted no woman. I never believed anything they were telling me. I was too aggressive. I would punch doors, wreck furniture, punch windscreens in cars. I just wasn't a nice person. The aggression within me was fierce. But there was a gentle side to me, a loving side, a caring side. I really liked that side of me. It was the real me. This aggressive person that had been manufactured was not the real me. It was hiding what was really going on underneath but at that time I never realised this.

I became very close friends with a guy called Billy. Billy was a close protection operative and taught martial arts and self-defence classes at our local gym. It's how I got to know Billy, through the gym. Me and Billy ignited a strong friendship, and one I completely respected. Myself and Billy got involved with car ringing, an old trait of mine and we became very good at it. I still worked the door at the Union Bar and during that time I became very close friends also with a guy called Dave Trimble, a 6-ft 7 ex-Scots Guards, who had served in the Falklands war. This man feared no man. He was quiet, he was polite, he was courteous and relaxed, but at the flick of a switch he would be a raging animal, totally uncontrolled - something I'd never seen before. Only once had I seen Dave flip like this and that's when we worked together at Zoots nightclub when a large group of guys kicked off. This was a big off; there were only four of us working that night. Billy was one of them. We were totally outnumbered but we did what we could and dealt with the situation.

The one vision I had when I looked over to the corner of the bar was, I could see Dave cornered by a group of guys and he was there in his rage trying to smash a champagne bottle on the counter, shouting, "Come on, then." That was a split vision of a split second as I was trying to pull a DJ off the floor from a beating. So, I knew what Dave was capable of and I loved the man. He was so kind and just a humble time bomb, and I liked that.

Myself and Billy became close and continued with that car ringing. We weren't earning fortunes but it paid the bills. But life was about to change severely. I was dating a girl but I wasn't a nice person, still aggressive, still steroid-induced, still punching doors, losing my temper, taking drugs, selling drugs. Violence - you name it, it was happening.

I got into a little bit of acting work through a friend and thought I'd try my hand at acting, not sure why I fancied this as I wasn't a very outgoing person but it was something new. It was something that didn't involve violence and drugs or aggression. It was mild, it was happy, and meeting a new variety of people was exciting. I attended evening theatre school and enjoyed it. With a view to obtain an agent, I attended an interview with a guy called Ray Knight in North London. He was a casting agent and I immediately clicked with this guy. I had created a portfolio and managed to get a few little jobs which led me to an acting role in a TV series called 'Broker's Man' starring Kevin Whately.

As it happened, despite walking away from violence and trying my hand at something mild-mannered, they gave me a role as a debt collecting violent skinhead. Fantastic! I immediately felt typecast. But I had so much fun and remember sitting in the chair in the makeup room next to Kevin Whately, loved this new journey. This was my new direction, this was where I wanted to go. It was fun, it was relaxed. I enjoyed it and meeting people from another walk of life away from the world I'd been accustomed to. But this was all about to change dramatically to a level I could never have imagined. The police started to have an interest in me and a very serious interest at that. This was a degree of police interest which took my whole life to a different level which would ruin the rest of my life.. This was a nightmare beyond all measure.

Chapter 4

My Trusting Heart

The early hours of one morning, the front door of the property I was living in was being knocked excessively hard. This was a knock that sounded very familiar, that familiar knock sounded official. I looked out of my bedroom window and witnessed groups of people and dogs which were not looking friendly. I put on my clothes, got dressed and walked down the stairs to open the door. It was the police with a very official presence.

I was read my rights and was arrested for questioning, regarding a shooting. This was something I knew nothing about or had any involvement with at all. I was hand cuffed and taken away. There must have been at least fifteen men and four dogs that entered my house to be searched. My life flashed before me. I was placed in a police cell stripped of my belt and shoes, and spent hours in there, before I was questioned. Whilst I sat in that police cell I wondered why, what shooting? I had no idea about this at all, no knowledge, nothing. This completely took me by surprise.

Eventually I was questioned not just once but several times over 36 hours. The police deliberately left my light on in the cell at night so I couldn't sleep. They used every tactic in the book, in every possible way to try and drain me, continuously questioning me, cross-examining me, asking me questions about a shooting I knew nothing about. I strongly had my suspicions my name had been put forward and the police were just following enquiries. I had no information to give. I had no knowledge of anything. I was asked where I was at the alleged time of the shooting which I gave. I had an alibi which the police checked out and was confirmed. I was nowhere present at the alleged time in the place of the shooting. I was looking at a life in prison for something I didn't do, something I knew nothing of and was not involved with in any way, shape or form. But it appeared my name had been put forward as information received.

Whilst sitting in the police cell I felt beaten. I was feeling robbed of a life and looked at life in prison, for something I knew nothing about. One thing for sure was whoever put my name in the frame I hope they rot in hell. It appeared my friend, Billy, was also arrested and questioned before me. Billy was eventually released after which they had to release me, too, which took me by surprise as I was expecting remand. However, there was no real case to answer and it appeared the police needed to look like they were doing something. I was placed in a paper suit and all my clothes were taken with my DNA and saliva sample.

I returned home to find my complete home stripped. It appeared the carpets had been pulled up, the floorboards had been pulled up, wall sockets taken out, all my clothes taken, the police had stripped my life. I was not allowed to confer with Billy, as it was a police requirement. I had no contact with him at all. All of a sudden, the press had an interest in me, The Sun newspaper knocking on my door, asking me for an interview. I refused and wanted nothing to do with the national press as I knew how twisting they could be.

The only evidence here they had was hearsay speculation, nothing substantial. It was an extremely weak arrest but one that hung over me. I was a suspect of a shooting which I knew nothing about. This was possibly the worst thing that could ever have happened, and for Billy, too. I had strict conditions. I was followed everywhere, my phone was tapped, my house was bugged a lot. This was a world that wasn't part of my journey and was never meant to be but it was about to haunt me for the rest of my life.

My head was in a complete mess, everything around me was falling apart and I mean, everything. The girl I was seeing, that relationship was going wrong, the pressure of life was getting to me, the police presence was strong. I was no gunman. Yes, I had a bad temper but shooting someone is another level and I was not on that level, never have I been, never will be.

The national press said that I did not want to comment as I didn't want to incriminate myself. I never said anything of the sort. What a thing to write! But I wouldn't expect anything less from the national press. It was very difficult to get back to any form of normality. I thought I would pop in and see my mum to see how she was handling this. She smiled, she came across ok but I could tell it was playing on her mind. She was devastated.

I told my mother I knew nothing of this shooting and I hoped that she believed me and she knew her son was not capable of shooting anyone. I gave my mum a cuddle and reassured her that things would be alright and not to worry. Some days later I received a telephone call from my solicitor stating all had been dropped on Billy and me. This was the news I had been waiting for and hoping for. The very first thing I did was call my mother and tell her the news. She was elated, she was so pleased and relieved, as was I too. I contacted Billy and he was over the moon and his family too, and agreed we just get on with normal life the best way we could, take time out from things and spend it with family. No arrests took place or further charges pressed on anyone. The case was left open.

The fear of serving a life sentence for something you didn't do, and that goes for either of us, was the scariest moment of my life. It truly was. As for my dear mother she was put through hell and that was one thing I never wanted to do. Heaps of my friends were questioned about me and they all said the same thing - Clive is not like that. This had done a lot of damage to me, a tremendous amount of damage. Mentally I was a mess, a very weak mess. I would spend hours crying. I was not in a good place. I was broke, I had no money, most certainly no prospects now and most certainly no life. I was ruined physically and mentally.

Where do I go from here, how am I going to live and certainly pay my bills? The house I was renting was off a friend called Eddie Phillips who lived in Rainham, Kent. This was Billy's cousin. I had been renting the house for some time. I hated it there, it had a bad vibe. I wanted to get out, especially after the police had invaded my private space.

My home felt dirty. I went back to work on the club doors in order to get some money together and start to live again. I was struggling badly. I became very close friends with my friend, Dave, 6-ft 7 ex Scots Guards Falklands veteran, who worked the nightclub doors with me. We became very close friends, a friend I really respected, he looked after me during the time of the shooting accusation. Dave was a real, true friend.

One particular day Eddie came to visit me with a proposition. This proposition was to rob a nightclub. This nightclub I had worked at for over two years, was notorious for drugs, notorious for the doormen selling drugs within the club, that I knew for sure. I knew that a lot of the drug money was kept in a safe and I knew the system within the club specifically the security layout and also the time of cashing up.

The owner of the nightclub was a horrible little man; I never liked him, a little Maltese man. And he used to pay us all in used £5 notes to make it look like he was paying us more money; a greedy, little Maltese man. I very much disliked him. The offer to rob the club was one I seriously considered. I truly needed the money and was willing to take the risk. Eddie said he had a friend that he wanted me to work with. His name was George. He said he was a good friend and one he trusted. I trusted Eddie.

I said to Eddie, "Give me some time to think about it." This was something totally out of my league but I was broke and in a very bad place. I had bills to pay. I was struggling in more ways than one. The offer was one I couldn't really turn down. I did think it odd that within days Eddie had approached me especially after having the investigation dropped against me regards a shooting. I did think everything was a bit strange but maybe I was just being paranoid.

I popped to the cemetery to see my father, looked at his grave, looked at the wooden cross which was all we could afford and I thought to myself, I have really let my father down. What happened to the promise I made to his wife, my mother? What has become of me and where was I going with my life? My prospects were not looking good and I knew that my mum was still paying for a funeral she couldn't afford. We could not even afford a headstone for my father's grave. Things were really bad. I put my hand on my father's cross and promised him I would try my best whatever the cost and promised him one day he would have a headstone for his grave. I had made a lot of promises, one to look after my mother, one for a headstone. Could I keep these promises? I hated breaking promises and the consideration to rob the nightclub became strong. At that point I had made my mind up and would contact Eddie to try and make plans to commit a robbery on the club. After contacting Eddie, we set a date for a meeting to plan the robbery. After a number of days, Eddie made arrangements for me to meet George and Paul. Eddie said, "I'm just going to make the introduction to you. It's down to you guys to just give me a drink when it's done."

A meeting was arranged between me and George in the fire exit of the nightclub in which I was working on that Saturday night. Something kept telling me, give him a body search, a gut feeling was telling me to check him over for a wire. I don't know why my instincts were telling me this but I wanted to buzz him over. This was something that was told to me many years ago go by a very good friend of mine. He used to say DTA, "Don't trust anyone." The meeting was arranged for 9 p.m. that night at the rear of the nightclub in the fire exit. I had drawn a plan of the security layout of the nightclub. The drawing was a detailed account of the area where the safe was kept, details of the time of cashing up and the time all the doormen would leave the reception area, which would have been approx. 3:30 a.m.

At the first meeting, George came across as if he was an east end villain, mid 50s, with a stubble, a very deep voice and a way about him that just said, villain, very convincing. The body search never happened but from that point on robbery was being planned. He said he would do the job with his friend Paul whom I would meet at a later date. George said this needed to be an armed robbery preferably shotgun and handgun and could I get hold of these. I didn't want to appear a weak link. I said I would look into it.

This was our first meeting, one of about several. At the second meeting I was going to meet Paul who was his partner in crime as such. After the meeting with George I returned back to the nightclub door with a million thoughts running through my mind and mainly the one to make sure my mother would be ok financially and put a headstone on my father's grave. That was all I was worried about and hoping there will be enough left over from the robbery to help me out a little.

What had I become, who am I, what am I? Is this the real me? What's become of me, after years of being taunted by a nasty horrible person. On assessment of myself I had become that person. I was that nasty horrible person, violence, robberies, car theft. What did my life look like from an outsider's view? I started using drugs, mainly cocaine and Speed. This became my weekly fix which would normally take me the week to recover. I was not in a good place, mentally I was far from it. I was in a very bad place, a very dark place and a place I've never been before, scrambling for survival.

I was that little brat which I was told I was. I had become that person. The violence on the club doors became regular. My tolerance was less. The drink and drugs masked my real feelings and the drugs became my friend, a friendly enemy, one that loved me despite my faults. Whilst on drugs I felt a different person. It lifted my fears, restored my confidence and put me at the top of the game where I felt strong.

At this point I started talking to my sister again. After some years of her not talking to me we regained our relationship at which my mother was very pleased and relieved that we did. I had my doubts, I had my fears, I had my worries, but it was what my mother wanted and if it made her happy, it made me happy. The police was making a regular presence around me. I regularly had unmarked police cars parked outside my house. On one occasion I walked out of my house and offered the police cups of tea. They declined and drove away. I laughed. I just needed to let them know I was aware of their presence.

I received a physical visit from two men in suits. I opened the door and to my surprise two police officers wanted to talk to me. I asked them what it was about and they asked to come in for a chat. I reluctantly let them. They said to me they were investigating a murder, a shooting down of a man down a country lane, early hours of one morning. I looked at them in horror, in disgust and said to them, "Are you having a laugh or are you for real?" They proceeded to give me the name of the guy whom I had heard of, I never knew personally. A road cone had been placed outside his gate. It appears as the man pulled up in his car he had to get out to remove the cone and at that the gunman shot him.

They asked me where I was at the alleged time of shooting. I told them I was working at the club as security in Maidstone which I did not leave until the very early hours for which I had witnesses - management staff, door staff, everyone. Once again, I knew nothing of this, no involvement, and being accused of being a contract killer was unbelievable, beyond words. What the hell was happening? Who was putting my name forward all the time, why is my name coming up every time someone gets shot? The finger seems to get pointed at me. This was becoming a joke. I'd had enough of the police and their accusations. The aggression got fierce within me.

My alibi was checked out and once again proved it could not have been me at all. This did not phase me out from planning the armed robbery. Life could not get any worse. I felt I had nothing to lose. My mother was struggling to pay her bills. She was working in a café, washing dishes, totally broke and skint. My objective was to pull in as much money I could from the robbery which George and Paul committed. My job was just the information man, that's all I was. I asked my big friend, Dave, if he wouldn't mind coming to meetings with me with these guys as I needed a little bit of muscle if things went wrong.

Various meetings took place and Dave came with me just for a little security, that's all. At my first meeting with Paul I was a little unsure, but was it the drugs that was making me paranoid? I wasn't in a good place mentally.

Throughout the meetings with George and Paul they insisted they wanted me to supply the firearms for the robbery. I said I had made enquiries. The truth of the matter was, I had no idea where to obtain them. I had no contacts for firearms. This was not my world, it's a place I'd never been in before. I've never held any firearms or had any in my possession, but I didn't want to look like a little frightened boy. I played the big man and kept them hanging on, but their constant persistence for firearms started to ring alarm bells within me. I began to get suspicious. Things were not ringing right. I said to Dave,

"What's your opinion on these guys?" In his own words, it was, "I don't trust them."

I started to feel something wasn't right. Why were these guys aggravating me to supply them with firearms? What was it? I kept questioning it. I was extremely paranoid on the best of days, this was making me worse. On one particular occasion I decided to turn up early for one of the meetings prior to George and Paul arriving for our meeting. A marked police car drove past me. Then directly behind were George and Paul. This confirmed my suspicions. Was it a coincidence? Was it my paranoia? It didn't seem right.

I kept my thoughts close to my chest and took on board what Dave felt too. But I still believed it was my paranoia getting the better of me. I had a backup plan if things would go wrong on the robbery. It was getting close to the date of the robbery, and George and Paul once again asked me for firearms. I declined, I said 'no', I stood firm and told them that's their job. I wanted no involvement in firearms or obtaining them at all. They are the robbers. I'm just the information man for the job. That's all I wanted to do.

The night of the robbery was close but the police presence around me was strong. In fact, it got stronger constantly, followed constantly, stopped, constantly harassed. I suspected my phone was bugged and the house. All this didn't deter me from planning the robbery. I needed the money. My mother needed the money. She needed help. We had a funeral to pay for and a headstone to purchase. I had made a promise to my father as he lay there in that hospital, dead. That vision of my mother crying over the top of him would never leave me and the promise I gave to my father, no matter the cost, I would not break that promise and I would see this robbery.

The night before the robbery I sat with my mother and my exact words were, "Mum we're going to be alright and we're going to get a headstone for Dad." I gave her a kiss and a cuddle and assured her everything was going to be ok from now on.

Within my mind whatever was in that safe at the nightclub, I was going to get a very healthy percentage and that would cover the remainder of the funeral costs, to purchase a headstone and pay our bills and give us a little bit of a more comfortable time. Little did I know this was certainly not the case and was never going to be. At the time it was all I had to live for. Whatever the consequences I could not break the promise I made to my father, it was make or break. I had become this person I didn't like. I had become this person that my sister said I was, but deep down despite all this wrong I knew my heart was kind. Behind all the wrong decisions I ever made the motive behind them was for good reasons - the car ringing, the car theft that was all I was, and it was all I was ever going to be. I was a small-time crook, nothing more. I was not the person the police made me out to be. I was not the horrible person my sister made me out to be but I was convinced I was that person. If you're told something for so long you end up believing you are that person.

The night of the robbery was upon us. I drove past the nightclub with a view to check if the getaway vehicles were in place as agreed. I began to think my suspicions and my doubts of Paul and George being undercover police officers was down to my paranoia as this robbery was taking place, the getaway vehicles were in place where they said they were going to be -everything was in order.

But because I still had an element of doubt I had a backup plan which was a note; a letter in which I wrote, "I know I am subject to a police set up. I know I am being set up by the police. This is my note of evidence in order to prove I am being set up and being harassed." I decided to hide this note behind the washbasin in the bathroom of my house so if I was unlucky to be arrested this was my backup plan to prove I was being set up by the police while their objective was to find firearms that were used in shootings, and this was a complete police setup from the word 'go'. This was my back up plan and only time would tell if my suspicions were right.

At 3:45a.m. the robbery was going to take place. George and Paul were going to rob the nightclub, tie up the occupants and rob the safe, as not only were there the takings from the club, there were the takings from the drugs that were sold within the club which the management had full control over, so I knew there was going to be a lot more money than simply the club takings.

The agreement was, I would wait for George to call me once the robbery had been done and meet me to receive my percentage of the takings. The agreed meeting place was Farthing Corner services on the M2 coastbound. I knew the time of call would be approximately 4.15 am. I asked Dave to drive me to the meeting point but I asked him to drop me off and go home, so if things went wrong it would be just me that would be arrested not Dave. Dave was reluctant to leave me on my own but that was what I wanted. If anyone was going down it would just be me, and me alone. I got Dave to drop me to Farthing Corner services M20 after we had finished work at the nightclub on the door. I walked into the cafe facing the car park so I could have visual contact with the car park where I would wait for George.

I sat patiently and I waited for George's phone call. I finally received a call from George and he was on his way to meet me at Farthing Corner services. The conversation was short and brief. My emotions were mixed- anxiety, aggression, fear and excitement. This is it. I am saved and my family is going to be ok. It's actually happened. I thought of my mother with a smile, saying to myself, "You're going to be alright, mum, we're going to be ok. Just this one little job and I will never do anything like this again." It was way out of my league. It was never my thing but it was going to help us get straight, it was my only way. It was all I could have done at that time but we were going to be alright. I was pushed into such a corner after the constant police harassment. I needed the money badly.

I waited patiently until eventually I saw George and Paul arrive into the car park. I thought to myself, this is actually it. I got up, put my coffee down and left the building and walked towards the old beaten up Mondeo that George and Paul were driving. I opened up the rear door and jumped in the back of the car and a conversation took place. My excited thoughts were, my life was about to change for the better. Paul had pulled out a bag. Within this bag there were bundles of money wrapped very neatly, and within that bag was my proceeds, my percentage of the robbery. George in his very deep voice said to me everything went according to plan, everything was spot on, and he tied them up and cleaned the safe out and there was my cut from the robbery. I assumed they would give Eddie his cut as he was their contact, not mine.

Something wasn't right. How could they have put all the notes together so neatly, all in bundles of thousands as the cash would not be sitting in the safe like that so neatly wrapped with elastic bands. But I took the money put it inside my jacket, shook hands with George and Paul and said, "Thanks guys until next time." We laughed and said our goodbyes.

But that was not the end. As I looked around me there were cars screeching all around me - police cars, unmarked cars, vans - you name it, it was around me. I was asked to get out of the vehicle. With that, there was armed police surrounding me. They asked George and Paul to get out of the vehicle, hands in the air and to get on the floor. All three of us got on the floor but I looked around to George and my exact words were, "You're f****** old bill, aren't you? You've set me up, the lot of you set me up, you dirty bastards." They pulled George and Paul off the floor and pulled me up off the floor put my hands behind my back, handcuffed me and took the money from inside my jacket. My heart sank, my world crashed before me, truly stamped on, pure devastation. My life flashed before me. My suspicions were right. It wasn't paranoia, it was a police setup and my thoughts were correct, the continuation of being harassed by the police. They had gone out of their way to set me up to locate firearms that would possibly be used in shootings.

They had set me up. I was thrown in the back of the Mondeo, handcuffed. The sun was just coming up, the morning was dawning, and I knew I was on my way to prison. My initial thoughts were of my mother, it's over, it's totally over. There was no getting away from this but my backup plan, my little note stating I've gone through with this to prove how low the police would go to put me away and get me off the streets with dirty tactics to find firearms that were thought to be used to shoot people. A dirty crafty tactic - how could they do this to me, how are they allowed? But my little note was my evidence to prove harassment and show the levels the police would go to. My heart was broken. The promise I made to my father was broken. I had let everybody down including myself - what was I thinking? My little note that I left behind the bathroom wash basin was potentially my saviour.

Chapter 5

The Tears of a Heart Broken Mother

I t was the usual routine - shoes off, belt off, placed in a police cell to awake to questioning - the usual routine after being arrested. Once all signed in, you're placed in your concrete room where you will sit and wait for hours to be questioned regarding your arrest. This had become a very regular occurrence for me but I was about to set myself to get used to this for some years. The thoughts of my mother were racing through my mind, a million thoughts were racing. I could not get my mother out of my mind. I was hoping that my backup plan, my hidden note behind the wash basin in the bathroom was my get out clause, so to speak. I was not going to lie; apart from my paranoia, I was so hoping the robbery was real that the people that Eddie introduced me to were real villains. I trusted the man, had no reason to mistrust at all, however it was clear Eddie had introduced me to two undercover police officers. I was incited into a manufactured crime to obtain firearms which the police assumed I may have had from shootings, guns that I'd never seen, never held, never likely to and never would have done. But Eddie had introduced me to two undercover police officers, that was fact.

The question I kept asking myself, why would Eddie do this to me, what was his objective to do this to me, to set me up, introducing me to undercover police officers, what was in it for him? My mind was racing a hundred miles an hour. The only concern I had was my mother.

It's normally hours before you're seen and questioned by the police. I was offered a cup of tea which I accepted and one of their horrible, dry microwaved breakfasts which also I accepted. But sitting there for hours gives you a lot of time to think, a hell of a lot of time to think why was I setup and what was Eddie getting out of this? Was Eddie a police informant? But I thought that can't be right, surely not, as Eddie had a reputation for being a professional criminal in many ways. Was I just being paranoid again, should I be using my paranoia as logic? All the paranoid thoughts that I have had were correct. Not just the drugs, not just the come down, it just highlighted what was really happening to me and as the saying goes, always follow your gut instinct and that's something I should have done.

Eventually the police came to get me for questioning for which I had been waiting, to spring my backup plan on them, but I know for sure they would have searched my home once again. I prayed they did not find my hidden note, my backup plan to reveal I had been set-up, harassed, which was the truth. From the moment I was accused of shooting people, the police did not leave me alone.

The interview tapes were being set up and I was read my rights - "Clive Sands, you have been arrested on suspicion of conspiracy to commit armed robbery. You do not have to say anything, but it may harm your defence if you do not mention, when questioned, something which you may rely on in court." Questioning took place which lasted. It felt as if it was for days. I waited for them to proceed with all the evidence that they had against me. All my meetings with George and Paul were recorded, photographs of meetings, recordings of meetings -everything was recorded. Of course, George and Paul were pseudonyms, not their real names.

They proceeded to explain to me that Dave had also been arrested and was now about to be questioned regarding the armed robbery. I said to them that Dave had no involvement, he was only driving me to the meetings to look out for me. He was not part of the robbery, obtaining no proceeds from the robbery. He had no involvement whatsoever regarding the robbery. However, they proceeded to tell me that Dave was party to the meetings which made him part of the conspiracy of the robbery. That broke my heart as Dave did not deserve to be arrested. He only looked out for me, he was not part of the robbery. I was devastated for him. Dave's voice was on all the recordings during the meetings with George and Paul, also photographs of Dave with me, with George and Paul - everything was monitored and recorded.

The only person that was not monitored and recorded, no photographs or anything, was Eddie. Eddie was not mentioned at all, nothing was spoken about Eddie and his involvement and introduction of George and Paul. Eddie was not talked about, Eddie was not mentioned in any way, shape or form, yet he was part of the introduction to rob the nightclub. He was not arrested, he was not part of the questioning, nothing. This created massive suspicion over the whole robbery. Eddie was clearly the set-up man used by the police to incite me into a manufactured armed robbery. It was clear that Eddy was working for the police.

My blood was boiling to the point of realisation that Eddie must have been a registered police informant working on behalf of the serious crime squad. Dirty low life piece of scum, how could he do that to me? He was Billy's cousin, they were very close. My thoughts ran wild. Why had everybody targeted me, why was I the scapegoat? Is it just because I'm the easy target for everyone to put my name up?

I then proceeded to hit them my with my hidden note. I told them from the word 'go', from meeting George and Paul, that this was a police setup because I realised they were harassing me for so long, they wanted to get me off the streets, find the firearms that we used in shootings which I never had and were never in my possession as I had never attempted to shoot or kill anybody, yet the police targeted me, and me solely, me, nobody else, not Billy, not anybody, just me and me alone. I was a marked man. Eddie was clearly working for the police. Everybody around me, all those that I cared for and loved and trusted, I felt, were letting me down. I was fuming but was hoping that my backup plan, my hidden note behind the bathroom wash basin was my saviour.

They looked very shocked, in fact, worried because there was no way whilst in police custody I could have placed or let anybody know to place that letter behind the washbasin. It was clearly put there before I was arrested. This was my get out clause and I was praying that it was going to save me.

I was placed back in my police cell where I sat for a further four maybe six hours whilst they returned back to my home to find the hidden note behind my wash basin. I prayed that this would save me. My head was running wild, stressing and worrying, anticipating, frightened, crying, sadness - you name it, every single emotion ran through my veins with anger at Eddie for setting me up and putting me behind bars for a considerable number of years.

Yes, I broke the law trying to put food on the table, just a small-time crook. Nothing like I was being portrayed as. I wanted to help my mother, but I went about things the completely wrong way. The robbery was well out of my league, it wasn't something that would have ever interested me.

I knew I was going to prison. I wanted to contact Billy to let him know about Eddie, how his cousin was a dirty police informant. However, this was a bit difficult for me to do because I knew I was going to be placed on remand, that was inevitable. A little while later I was placed back in the interview room for questioning. The police presented me in a clear plastic envelope with my letter showing in detail that I knew I was subject to police harassment and set up by the police.

Throughout questioning they asked me why did I go through with it if I knew the police was setting me up, and my reply was I needed to prove, 'how much you were harassing me, the length you all went to, by following me, bugging my phones, bug in my house, constant harassment - why me? Why was I the only one targeted throughout, and nobody else, just me?' I asked the police that question at which they completely blanked and then I proceeded to ask them, "Why wasn't Eddie arrested? Is Eddie your police informant? And did Eddie set me up along with George and Paul?" All the police basically said to me was they could not confirm or deny that Eddie was a police informant, but that was good enough for me because clearly all meetings were recorded, photographs were taken. Dave was arrested, also no photos or recordings of Eddie the main man of the robbery, the man that introduced us was not arrested, was not questioned. This was clear cut that Eddie was working for the police. They used Eddie to incite me into a manufactured crime.

Hours upon hours of questioning, and I knew poor Dave was also being questioned, was draining. Our problem was pointless, us going "no comment " when we were bang to rights. Voices are all on tape, planning an armed robbery. So really in a nutshell it was a clear-cut case. It appeared my note was to be taken into consideration and would be presented in court when a trial would take place in which I would be going 'not guilty' to conspiracy to commit armed robbery. Sadly, Dave was charged with conspiracy to rob along with myself, that was, charged with conspiracy to rob. The next step was obviously remand. Bearing in mind this was a Sunday, myself and Dave would be transferred to HMP Elmley in Sheerness where we both would be placed on remand awaiting trial. I was allowed one telephone call in which I called my mother and sadly broke the news to her, tears running down my face. I could not catch my breath, my heart and my soul ripped from my body as I heard her cry on the other end of the phone. She was absolutely, totally, devastated.

I had never been to prison before. I didn't know the procedure on how things work so, I explained to my mother I would call her at the next available time I could and let her know what was happening. Putting the phone down was one of the hardest things I'd ever had to do. It was heart-breaking; beyond heart-breaking - soul wrenching, hearing my mother cry as a result of my pure stupidity chasing something albeit for the right reasons - to put food on the table, to help my mother with the funeral costs and put a headstone on my father's grave.

On the following Monday morning, myself and Dave awaited transportation to HMP Elmley where we would be both placed on remand until we were given a trial date. I had never been in a prison van before. I was cuffed and walked with several prison officers to the prison van where I remained cuffed until I entered a small door with a small cubicle with a plastic chair and a very small window which was darkened. As I stepped into the plastic cubicle of the van, the prison guard released my cuffs and a door was slammed and bolted. I then saw Dave also assisted with various guards, all 6-ft 7 ex Scots Guard

Falklands veteran, was also placed into the plastic cubicle with the door slammed.

It was very difficult to talk to Dave. I didn't know what to say. I would plan to talk to him once we arrived at HMP Elmley. We drove off and proceeded to what would be my new home for possibly some years. The sun was shining, I could see the birds, I could see wildlife, I could see the trees, the wind blowing at the leaves, people walking, cars - day to day life was going on and mine had come to a screeching halt. Life as I knew it, was gone, and my new life in prison was about to start. My anger was fierce. Eddie was obviously working for the police and this had to be told throughout the prison system, people had to know what this local so-called villain had done and what he possibly had also done to others. It was very obvious that the police always left him alone. He had never really done any prison at all; if it was, it was just a few months to make him look authentic. But never for years; it all made sense.

As the prison van with myself and Dave within it approached Sheerness bridge a song came into my head. The song was by Robbie Williams, 'No Regrets'. As I looked at the sunlight beaming through my darkened porthole window I turned left to look at Dave whom I could just about see in the opposite cubicle with his head in his hands. I could see he was devastated and this was my fault. All he wanted to do was look out for me and come to the meets and keep me safe, and now he was possibly looking at years in prison for part of a conspiracy to commit an armed robbery on a nightclub which was set up, obviously by Eddie, a police informant. We were robbed of our freedom and I was harassed for things I never did.

That song 'No Regrets' was continuously running through my mind and my mother was now left to fend for herself, pay for a funeral on her own and survive. My mother was Italian and came into this country in 1952. She could hardly read or write any English and was dependent on others to help her with her bills. After my father passed away my mother really struggled. It was my duty as her son, as a promise I made to my father, to look after my mother, I had totally broken and this devastated me, truly devastated me and I would never forgive myself for the shame I brought to my mother.

41

As we approached the big gates of HMP Elmley I will never forget how those Gates opened as the van drove through it. Reality had hit. We went into a small section as the big gate shut behind us and we were placed into a cubicle area where obviously we would be let out of the van and escorted into the prison.

Dave was let out of his cubicle first and taken down into the holding cells, I assumed. Then the prison guards came to get me and took me into where there was an area where the cuffs were taken off, where I was about to be placed into prison clothing. My photo was taken and I was given a prison number - RN2790 was my prison number. I was placed into a caged area where other cons were sitting and there sat Dave. This was my first physical meeting with Dave since we were arrested and I apologised. I deeply apologised and felt so guilty as Dave was only driving me to the meetings to look out for me. He was no part of any robbery, however sadly due to the fact he was on tapes as we were recorded on all the meetings, it was difficult and showed he was involved in conversations about the robbery which were clearly taped recordings by the police. I said to Dave we had been set up, mainly myself being the target. I proceeded to tell Dave that Eddie had not been arrested. His first initial reaction was, "You're joking, he introduced you to everyone, he was the one that came to you about the robbery."

I said to Dave I knew now Eddie was clearly an informant working for the police as I knew Eddie was up on other charges at the time and obviously those charges were most likely dropped as most informants get away with everything, provided they give the police information on other villains which clearly Eddie did and, most likely, the police used Eddie to get to me.

There was a guy opposite us that had been arrested too for something else and also being placed on remand. He overheard our conversation about Eddie and said he knew Eddie. Eddie had been known to be a police informant for around ten years. This guy's name was Mark. We connected straight away and talked about Eddie and what he knew about being a registered police informant. This blew my mind. I paced up and down whilst Dave sat down, also fuming, absolutely fuming. Mark proceeded to tell us that Eddie was getting away with a lot of crime and had been for some years, and that amongst the criminal fraternity he was known as a 'grass'.

Then why didn't Billy tell me about this? Did he know? I wasn't sure about anything, I was struggling to believe and trust in anything and anyone. Myself and Dave were in complete devastation. We waited to be moved to house block one where we would both be either in together or in separate cells. At that point I had no idea. Eventually we were moved. All I could recall was keys rattling as they entered the locks, the keys hitting the locks, the rattling of keys as the doors opened and slammed, and the echoes of the cons; the smell, the atmosphere, was strange. The echoes were strange, it was a feeling and vision and a smell that would never leave me as we proceeded to walk onto house block one with our HMP bags, with our plastic knife, our plastic fork, and plastic plate and cup.

I was placed in a single cell and Dave was placed also in a three-up cell. The first night I will never forget, the echoes of the doors slamming, the keys rattling, the smell, the atmosphere. There were all types and breeds of criminals. Some in my opinion were just there for a roof above their head and that I could understand. This was going to be the first night of what I was to believe to be for many years; how many I just did not know and neither did Dave - our first night in prison.

As the weeks went on Dave explained he was going to try and obtain bail to organise affairs of his house and life. I said to him I wished him the very best and hoped he got bail and as the weeks went on he was fortunate enough to be released on conditional bail and curfewed. This was something I was considering but knew the police would want to put a stop to that, to have me back on the streets; wherever they got this perception of me from and why I was the victim.

Dave was released on conditional bail and I had made enquiries to see if it was possible for me also. My solicitor that I was using at the time was Kevin. He was a lovely guy explaining to me the only way I would obtain conditional bail was, if I had a security to be put up; for example, a friend that will put up an amount of money or house etc. to be released on conditional bail. I had already served three months' remand and was awaiting trial which could possibly take up to a year before I would receive a trial date. My very dear friends, Paul and Tanya, offered to put up security about which they spoke to my solicitor and a court date was arranged for me to obtain possible bail.

I was given a court date where I was asked to attend, and Paul and Tanya were present. This was so nice of them to offer, in effect taking a risk in putting up funds for me to be placed on conditional bail.

The judge had asked if it was possible to put up £5,000 security which Paul had ready on that very day. It made me smile when I realised he had £5,000 in cash in a Tesco carrier bag with his banana and lunch all combined. The judge asked if he had this present and Paul replied whilst holding up the bag of used notes in the air and said, "Yes." It tickled me and made me laugh to myself when I realised Paul had brought in a bag of cash to grant me bail. I love the guy and will never forget his help.

£5,000 was not what I was expecting. I would have thought it had been a lot more, but I think the police realised it was an exceptionally weak charge - one that stood no real threat to society as in effect no armed robbery had taken place or was ever going to take place. No firearms were retrieved, nothing., and no robbery had taken place. All I did was talk about a robbery, that was all I did. I honestly could not see the crime, but being released on conditional curfewed bail gave me a chance to fight my case, prepare my case and to look into the laws of inciting people into manufactured crimes. We are talking 1997. I had a lot of work to do, a lot of research to do because I wanted to prove this case, that if it was not for Eddie introducing me to undercover police officers this would never have taken place.

This now gave me a chance to fight a case. I had regular visits with my solicitor during which I was instructed as when I do go to trial to plead guilty to conspiracy to rob. I was shocked at this. I was explained if I was found guilty I would be looking at around 10 years or more in prison for this charge. I was bewildered and shocked how could that be when no crime had taken place. But the crime is conspiracy, my intention to rob the nightclub was there, and the planning of the nightclub showed my intention to conspire with others, which was Dave.

I later looked into cases of entrapment as my case was a clear-cut case of entrapment. I was incited into a manufactured armed robbery by undercover police officers and a police informant that was used, called Eddie. I could not conspire with those who, in my opinion, had no intention to rob. How is that a conspiracy if they were not going to rob the nightclub? But because Dave was present it appeared my conspiracy was laid on with others, namely, Dave there was my conspirator.

I wanted to fight a case of entrapment. My case was one I was going to go 'not guilty' and take the risk and fight a case of entrapment and show how the police completely targeted me, harassed me, accused me of shooting people, questioned me over a contract killing I knew nothing about - why? I was the target. My suspicions were, Eddie was feeding them information, totally incorrect information, and placing my name forward which is why he worked so closely with the police.

In error, highly confidential information was sent to my co-defendants' solicitors revealing the informant. This was sent in error. This gave the name of the informant. This gave the details of everything, revealed the complete set-up, this paperwork was sent in error. Sadly, the paperwork was not allowed to be used in court due to it being highly confidential information called 'public interest immunity'. The paperwork was protected and we could not use it. This paper work confirmed all my suspicions.

But I pursued a case of entrapment against the police and I was going to stand my ground and take the risk and go 'not guilty'.

During my time on conditional bail I made time with my mother. She was so pleased to have me around. She assumed that I could be home for good, I had a strong case against the police for harassment and entrapment. I could not apologise enough to my mother. I had let her down I had let my father down. I broke the promise I had made. I tried so hard to do the right thing. I could not get a job. Nobody would employ me especially after being accused of shooting someone. No one will come near me. I know my mother understood deep down that my intentions were honourable, I just went about them the wrong way. I made the most of the time I could for my mother as I was unsure of the time that I may have had left with her.

A trial date had been set which was intended to be a three-week trial in July during the summer. The day was upon us. The sun shining, my fate was in the hands of a jury. I had worked hard trying to understand the laws of entrapment and my intention to use it as a defence along with my letter of proof that was hidden behind my washbasin in the bathroom, to prove a case of harassment by the police. It appeared that George and Paul were Scotland Yard undercover police officers working closely in a unit within Scotland Yard. How the hell did Scotland Yard suddenly have an interest in me? But I had the case planned in my head. 'Not guilty' was my plea and so was Dave's and we were going to push for a case of entrapment. I parked my blue Ford Sierra in the car park whilst wearing a crisp suit, white shirt and blue tie. My conditions were not to have had any contact with Dave but of course we did on many occasions; we needed to. This trial was going to be a battle, make or break time.

The jury was sworn in. The Honourable Judge Croft was our judge. I looked over at the jury. I could see a multitude of people none of whom I recognised, but I recall all their faces one by one registered in my mind which I knew was never going to leave me for the rest of my life. It was obvious Eddie was never going to be called as he was the police informant behind the whole robbery. George and Paul were called and obviously myself and Dave in the dock. Myself and Dave entered our pleas - 'not guilty'. The trial began. George and Paul were placed behind a screen.

As I gave evidence I continuously pushed the message forward about the arrest over a shooting, a shooting that I did not commit or have any involvement with at all. I also pushed forward that I knew I was being set up and made the jury know that Eddie introduced us to George and Paul, the undercover police officers. It was a pure case of police harassment and entrapment.

I also made sure the Jury knew how severe the harassment was, constantly followed, constantly checked on, constantly accused of things I hadn't done and made sure the jury knew how much Eddie was a major part of the incitement of us - myself and Dave - into this armed robbery and made sure the jury knew why Eddie wasn't standing trial as he was clearly part of a conspiracy to commit an armed robbery on the nightclub, yet he was not standing trial.

The jury put a note across to the judge to ask if Eddie was a police informant. The Judge's reply was: "I cannot confirm or deny whether Eddy is a police informant." This answered all my questions once again. Secondly another note was put across to the judge and asked: "Is entrapment a defence in English law?" The Judge replied, "Entrapment is no defence in English law."

To my pure horror, why did my legal team have me battling a case of entrapment when entrapment was no defence in English law? Why had they put me through a three-week trial wrongly advised when entrapment is no defence in English law? At that point I knew we were going to be found guilty. Clearly the jury could see Eddie incited me and Dave into the armed robbery because he clearly wasn't standing trial when he was clearly mentioned throughout interviews as well as recordings, yet he was not standing trial. It was obvious he was an informant and it was clear that the jury could recognise this was a case of entrapment but because the judge had informed the jury that entrapment was no defence in English law I knew in my heart of hearts the jury would have to find myself and Dave guilty.

The jury went out to decide their verdict. Three hours passed, and myself and Dave were recalled to the dock for a verdict. The judge proceeded to say, "Have you come to a decision, do you find Clive Edward Sands guilty or not guilty?" The jury replied, "Guilty." My head dropped in shame. I looked across at my mother and I could see her crying, I could see her tears, all my friends shocked, my mother devastated and my heart broken. The judge then proceeded to ask, "Do you find David Robert Trimble guilty or not guilty?" "Guilty," was the reply.

Sentence was now to be passed by The Honourable Judge Croft, a man I would never forget for his words stuck with me for the rest of my eternal life. "Mr Clive Edward Sands, you are a diminutive criminal, you were clearly the leader by a mile and your calculated approach in the planning of the robbery was precise with considerable subtlety. You will therefore serve a sentence of 7 years." My head dropped, I looked across at my dear mother in tears and heartbroken and devastated. She had lost her son for several years, no support, no protection and a broken promise I made to my father. My sister never made any attempt to support me at court, the person she used to call me, that nasty horrible little boy. This was registered within my mind like a computer. I was programmed to be that person which I had become over the years of being told I was horrible - the bullying, the manipulation and intimidation of being a horrible little boy - it all came crashing on me and gave me the confirmation she was obviously right. Sentence was then passed for Dave, "Mr David Robert Trimble, you were clearly part of the conspiracy to commit robbery. However, due to your exemplary military record and your outstanding service to the British Army and your previous good conduct and record, I sentence you to 15 months in prison."

Throughout the trial I tried my very best to take the pressure off Dave and explained to the jury it was my fault that Dave was involved. He was only there as a driver. He wasn't there for any other reason nor received funds from the robbery. Nothing. He was just security to make sure I was ok. I tried my very best as I did not want him getting a similar sentence to mine as I knew deep down, it was me the police wanted off the streets, not Dave.

The horrible Judge Croft then proceeded to say those words that would also haunt me eternally: "take them down." Myself and Dave were led out of the court into the cells where we would await transportation back to HMP Elmley to serve our sentences.

Before we went we were allowed to see our loved ones behind the glass screen. I was taken to a small room with a thickened safety glass which must have been three inches thick. There my mother stood in tears with a couple of my friends. This was heart-breaking. I placed my hand on the toughened glass where she placed her hand on the other side. There was no contact. The glass was too thick but it was the closest I could get to my mother. I then proceeded to turn around to walk away. I looked at the devastation on my mother's face with the loss of her son and my heart breaking. That vision will never leave me for the rest of my life.

Myself and Dave were now awaiting transportation back to HMP Elmley where we would serve our sentences. On arrival at Elmley we went through the same procedure as before and were then placed back on house block one until we became categorised. Devastation is a word that was just not strong enough that day. I was placed in a single cell up on the three's and Dave once again in the three-up cell. They locked me away that night behind my steel door, the keys rattling; that stale smell of a prison cell, as the door shut behind me, was my moment of realisation. When I looked on my sentence sheet of 2559 days to serve, it hit home the length of time. This was my home for a number of years. On my right hand I wore my father's ring. I took the ring off and placed it on the table. I looked out of my prison window which only opened a matter of an inch or two. I could see in the distance the high wall, the barbed wire, the fences, the security cameras, and in the distance, beyond trees and clouds was Freedom - a freedom I was not going to see for a number of years for a crime that never happened. I cried, I truly cried. I sobbed my heart and my soul. The devil had won, and my sister's words haunting me: "a nasty horrible little brat". How true, what had I become, who was I? What was I? My childhood played on my mind as I cried for my father. I had let him down. I made a promise and I broke it and I let my mother down.

This was my home now as I looked into the distance through my cell window. Drawing all my fears, flashbacks of my childhood all came before me. When you are told you are something for so many years you end up believing you are that person. Indirectly you become that person. As a child your mind is a computer that's being programmed by the people around you. Your upbringing is the most important part of your journey into this world as a child. Love from the people called your family is paramount, it's essential; it's the building blocks to your character. Take that away and you have nothing other than the path that has no direction, no purpose or fulfilment. I had become the person that I was told I was. This was now my journey - it was fight or flight.

Chapter 6

The Echoes of the Prison Walls

"TV thug a real jailbird" - The News of the World newspaper. Thanks to the National press for their lovely write up on me with along with a youthful photo of myself and actor Kevin Whately. This was a little write up on my very short acting career, one that was never destined to be and was never going to be. However, it was fun at the time. During bang up there was a little system of talking to your next-door neighbour in the next cell, and that was talking through the pipe. The majority of cells have a heated pipe that runs at the bottom of every wall underneath your window. It's very large in diameter and it's what keeps the cell warm during the winter. What cons do is put their face close to the pipe and shout to it which can echo through the steel pipe and which you can hear in the adjacent cell. I heard a heavy banging which was ringing through my pipe in my cell. The guy in the next cell was shouting to me, "Mate you're in the News of the World." I shouted back, "What about? The robbery?" I replied with laughter. It didn't surprise me, it didn't shock me, but I hoped that was the last reminder.

As the days and weeks passed, as the seasons passed into the months, the adjustment was difficult into prison life. I had no choice but to get used to it. My mother was on my mind daily. I received a letter from my mother in her broken English handwriting which thankfully I could understand. As you go through the system as a con you obtain privileges. I still was not due those yet. Being a long-term prisoner, I had a long way to go before I gained any privileges. Time was slow as expected. Dave had just months to serve which I was so pleased with. He was due to move to a Category D prison. As regards to myself I had to work my way through the system. There were years in front of me before I could be considered for anything.

I missed my mother terribly and the concern of her surviving, it was a deep worry. My sister moved to Kent from London to be closer to my mother, which did give me some comfort during my prison term. As the months slowly passed I was offered a transfer to HMP Coldingley in Surrey which was a working prison where you could earn £20 to £30 per week, which was something I seriously considered as I had no funds coming in. My mother had no money to send in for my spends, for items like decent toiletries, decent razors and general foods like tins of tuna and packet noodles which was the prison way of life.

I spent the majority of my time in either a single cell or a double which was on house block five at HMP Elmley. House block five was double cells which I had to share with another inmate, which I wasn't keen on but thankfully I was blessed with a decent guy that just liked to play chess which is where I learnt how to play. I managed to spend a little bit of time with Dave. I still felt very guilty for him even being there. He should not have been serving any prison sentence at all. He had lost his home, his job, everything, just to look out for me on those meetings. We both decided to apply to appeal against our sentences. Dave was advised not to bother, but I'm not one for giving up. It was a police setup. Despite entrapment not being a defence in English law I wanted to make my stand.

My first few months at HMP Elmley were slow which was to be expected. I managed to get a job on the gardens where at least I could get some fresh air. On one particular day one of the screws came to get me and said to me that I had a legal visit. I asked, "What legal visit? Is it my solicitor regarding my appeal?" He said "no," he didn't believe it to be so. I was curious and slightly concerned that if it's not my solicitor then who is it? I got changed and proceeded to be taken by one of the screws to the legal visit. On arrival, my solicitor was present and took me into a small room where could we could talk. He proceeded to tell me that the police had found other evidence on me regarding leaked information on a police informant and my fingerprints were found on the leaked documentation. I asked, "What information is this?" He then explained it was regarding a registered police informant. My first initial thought was Eddie, however it appeared not to be. It was leaked information on a well-known name, it was the son of a well-known London villain. There was a code name on this leaked information.

I kept quiet until I entered the room where two plain clothes police officers sat in front of me with my solicitor present. The police proceeded to ask me questions. "Have you ever been in possession of highly confidential information that was leaked from New Scotland Yard regarding a certain police informant?" I proceeded to say, "I know nothing of what you're talking about." They pulled out a document which was shown in a clear plastic envelope on which there was red dye of fingerprints on the documentation.

The police proceeded to ask me how my fingerprints had been found on this documentation which was leaked some time ago. My fingerprints were noted to be in a red dye. My prints were the only set of prints on this documentation. The police obviously were not settled with the result that they got, they were still on my case and not leaving me alone. They had already given me seven years for a robbery that didn't even take place. Now they wanted me arrested for something else on information, highly confidential information that had been leaked from New Scotland Yard on a notorious London crime family's certain son who was a registered police informant and my fingerprints were all over this documentation.

I proceeded to ask, "This information must have passed through various criminals' hands, how come there is only one set of prints? Obviously, this is leaked information and would have a number of fingerprints. Only one set of prints have been found on this paperwork and it appears to be mine."

Deep within my mind I knew that I had read this paperwork sometime previously along with so many others. I had handled this before. However, there were various copies made of this leaked information. That particular document was the original document.

I proceeded to tell the police, "I find it very hard that you only have one set of fingerprints bearing in mind this is a sort of paperwork that would fall into the hands of many villains, yet you only find one set of prints and it appears to be mine." I then told the police I had nothing further to say regarding this matter and asked to be returned back to the cell as I knew the police could not do an awful lot about this as someone within Scotland Yard had leaked this information on a very well-known face, the son of a well-known crime family. I knew there wasn't much that could be done as it was an embarrassment this information was leaked from Scotland Yard.

The police did not charge me or arrest me and to be brutally honest I wasn't even bothered if they did. I spoke to my solicitor thereafter and agreed the police did not want to appear to have egg on their face and it wasn't much the police could possibly do regarding this issue.

It just appeared the police was still on my case. Yes, I had read this paperwork before, yes, it had been in my possession before. I got deeper into the criminal world. It wasn't a place I wanted to be in as I didn't trust the majority of villains at all. In fact, I wasn't a very trusting person at all especially after what Eddie had done to me. Pretty much most of the time I was off my face on drugs. My paranoia was not of a trusting nature, the comedowns were fierce and dark. I returned back to the cell to carry on with my sentence and awaited my transfer date to HMP Coldingley to finally get my head down and crack on.

My very dear friend, Steve, wrote to me and said he was going to bring my mother up for a visit and could I send a visiting order which I did immediately as I could not wait to see my mother. I missed her so much. Daily she was on my mind and I needed to see her in person, to just hold the hand of my dear mother would be lovely. My friend, Steve, was like a brother to me, he was ten years older than me. We were a couple of naughty boys. Yes, we stole cars, yes, we ringed cars and sold them on, we were harmless small-time crooks and never hurt anyone. We just tried to make a few quid for our families.

I was granted my transfer to HMP Coldingley and was given a date for the 9th of November which was my transfer date. I needed a change of scenery from HMP Elmley. It was full of short-term prisoners always talking about the outside. At that point I was fed up of the plastic gangsters wearing their white Reebok Classics, the cocky swagger. Every one of them had villas in Spain, big time plastic gangsters. This type of villains was not my type of company. I needed to be in a long-term prison with long-term prisoners that were not constantly talking about the outside and their pathetic lives on how rich they were. These were not my kind of people at all.

I managed to get one visit whilst at HMP Elmley. My mother, my sister and Steve came to visit me. I will never forget that moment as I walked out of the visits area to proceed to walk towards my mother. She stood up from her plastic chair and looked over at me and smiled. The visit was electric, it was fulfilling spiritually, my beautiful mother that I had left behind, my beautiful mother that was struggling to pay her bills and living day to day, today was before me. My sister was there present. She had now moved to Kent. At least my mother had company and someone to be around her. The first thing my sister said to me, "You have lost a lot of weight, haven't you? Wish I was as skinny as you." She knew exactly what to say to wind me up, she just had to have that little dig at me. I was on rationed food, eating next to nothing in the situation I didn't want to be in and my sister made me feel even worse reminding me how much weight I'd lost due to the stress, anxiety and depression that I never realised I was suffering from.

Steve was so pleased to see me. We shook hands and said, "Good to see you, mate." That made my day, seeing Steve. Seeing my sister made me feel uneasy. Every time I saw her face, I could see her snarling face that would always look over me, belittling me, making me feel inadequate in life like she always had done.

The visit with my mother and Steve was beautiful. It had set me up for the next few months until I saw them again. I could see the sorrow in my mother's eyes, the Sadness, it was something that would never leave me. We as a family were not a loving family, we never really showed love. My father struggled to show me he loved me, but he had done it in his own way which now as an older man I see all so clearly now. My mother wasn't a very loving, cuddly mother, but I believed she loved me in her own way too. I managed to have a cuddle, I just wanted to hold her. I put on a brave face to make sure she knew I was ok, but I was broken inside, truly broken. Before I blinked an eye, the visit was over. As I walked away after saying my goodbyes, looking back at my mother it just broke my heart. I only ever wanted to do the right thing. I know I went about things the wrong way. I understand that now. As a child, growing up, I wasn't shown love, I didn't understand love. I knew what it felt like to feel the anxiety of not being wanted. All I wanted was love, all I wanted to do was love my mother along with sister and my father. I just wanted to love everybody and for them to love me equally the same. I went back to my cell. I was a broken soul, but at least I saw my mother. Thanks to Steve for bringing her up, a true diamond of life and a kind soul.

The 9th of November was upon me and it was my transfer date to HMP Coldingley. I bid my farewells to Dave and said, "When you get out mate, pop up and see me." We shook hands as I knew that was probably the last time I was going to see him for a few years. As you go through the system you realise what you're entitled to - parole - which was my aim. At least that gave me a little bit of light at the end of my tunnel and hoped I had a chance of parole if I simply got my head down, kept myself to myself and just got on with serving my sentence.

Whilst being transferred to HMP Coldingley, a really big African guy called Timothy Moses was being transferred with me. He was a huge guy with such a lovely presence. Back in that prison van again, it was actually a pleasure as we left HMP Elmley. It was nice to see the trees, the grass, cars, people walking, day to day, life, nature, dogs and cats; it was just lovely to see normal life. I'd only served approximately seven months of my seven-year sentence. It had felt like eternity but just to be travelling in what we call the "SweatBox" - it was a nice privilege to see normal life. I began to learn something very quickly, that isolation really didn't bother me. It really didn't affect me too much being locked up in a cell as when I had flashbacks of my childhood I had spent hours upon hours in my bedroom on my own, my place of safety, with the door shut. Prison, its isolation, being banged up as they call it didn't bother me, not at all. In fact, I liked it. Yes, it affected me. Of course, it would mean losing my freedom, but the isolation didn't.

Whilst travelling in the prison van flashbacks again of my childhood were very present. One thing prison does, it gives you time to think, time to think about your life. You think about your family, your childhood and where you have gone wrong in life. I call it discovery, and prison was going to teach me an awful lot about myself. Over a period of years prison can either make or break you. Many return. You have choice - learn from your mistakes, utilise prison properly and make sure you do not come back again.

Whilst being transferred to HMP Coldingley we stopped off at HMP Wandsworth. Now that is a real jail. Myself and Timothy were placed in the holding cells of HMP Wandsworth. We were not sure if this was some kind of setup where we were going to stay at Wandsworth or be moved on. We had the famous Wandsworth duff. Duff is a sponge pudding, size of a brick but actually it's quite nice with custard. Wandsworth duff was quite notorious.

We discovered it was just a break for some lunch before we were shipped to HMP Coldingley where our new cells were awaiting us. Timothy was a Christian, loved his church and had his faith and told me, "Trust in Jesus. He will see you through. Believe and have faith and you'll be fine." Those words stuck with me and will never leave me as deep down I had faith. I had been brought up in a strict Italian Catholic upbringing. I was surrounded by faith, my mother was a devoted Catholic, and her faith was her strength.

On arrival at HMP Coldingley it was the usual routine of being signed through reception with induction and eventually taken to your cells. Myself and Timothy were both on the same spur. I found this jail very dark, very old and very dated. I was given a small pot which is called a slop out pot, which is your toilet.

This seemed very draconian, something from the TV series 'Porridge', but that's jail for you. There was a very high volume of Jamaicans and Africans. They loved their Domino's which they were very passionate about. 'Yardies', very serious guys, but I love all breeds of people. There is good and bad in everyone in this world, and that's one thing I have learnt. I actually liked HMP Coldingley because they were all single cells, no double ups, all single cells. I was hoping to work my way through the system keeping my head down. I'm the quiet one that keeps himself to himself, picks and chooses company very carefully. Whilst there I bumped into an inmate that I had met at HMP Elmley; his name was Alfie. I loved the guy, mid 50s, sentenced for drug smuggling. I just loved him; old school old morals, just one of life's naughty people but with a good heart. We became very close friends.

I came across a man called Frankie Turpin from East London serving life for murder. He offered me a place in his workplace with other lifers, which I took. I loved being around lifers. They never talked about the outside. They just got on with their sentences, they were relaxed and chilled. This is what I need - to be around people that were relaxed and just getting on with their time. I became very close friends with Frank and the other lifers. One guy was called Duchy. He was 10 years over his tariff. He did not want to go home, he had met every conceivable notorious inmate throughout the system. Ronnie and Reggie Kray, Charles Bronson - he had met them all and he did not want to go home. He had his boyfriend, called Harry, and once again each to their own. I got on really well with Duchy. He was about 9 stone wringing wet. He was tiny with wild grey hair with that grey prison facial look that most lifers had. This guy did not care about or fear anyone. If you upset him he wouldn't have thought twice about slitting your throat; but that's his nature. But I got on well with him.

Whilst serving my seven years in HMP Coldingley I decided to write a book on my life. One thing I did have, and that was time, and a lot of it. I wrote to my sister to ask if she would be able to type my book up for me, and she replied she would be glad to help. In a way, this was my therapy - writing about my life, putting it down on paper, going through every emotion and feeling was something I needed to do at that time. All my experiences, from a child to the moment of prison, my loves, my fears, my tears, sadness, happiness, the lot.

After my talking to Frankie, he said he could introduce me to a guy that may be able to help me with regard to the publishing of my book. His name was Paul Ravilious. He was close friends with a guy called Stephen Richards who published various books of various people. This was a great contact for me. I wrote to Paul and bearing in mind everything takes weeks - I didn't have any access to a computer nothing so everything was handwritten - would wait weeks for replies from people. However, Paul did reply to me and we hit it off straight away. He sent me some amazing letters and became a very good pen friend. He said he had a lovely friend called Jan Lamb who was nicknamed, 'Angel of the underworld'. I knew nothing of Jan at that point. I was given her address. She could help me as she was part of some kind of reform for prisoners which also dealt with cases of miscarriages of justice. I thought this would be a great contact for me. Me and Jan, who also was an amazing lady, became very good friends. Ronnie Kray had asked to marry Jan some years before. She was obviously friends with some very high-profile faces. She was an amazing contact and had written various books. With her knowledge and experience this could be vital for me. I still had not had seen my mother since my last visit at HMP Elmley. It was Christmas 1999. My first Christmas in prison away from my family, specifically my mother. This was a very emotional time for me. On numerous occasions I would sit in my cell in tears, thinking - how did I get here? I was never meant to be this person. I wasn't this person deep down but I was here in my concrete room with my AM FM radio, my slop out pot under the bed, my small table and my pen and my paper which became my friend, my expression of my journey, which I would put down on paper with a view to write about my life and how I ended up here. The continuation of flashbacks of my childhood, being locked in a bedroom, where my sister instigated her friend to sexually assault me - that vision never left my mind ever, from the age of seven years old flashbacks of my sister and her treatment to me as a child.

One Christmas I recalled a memory. My sister was sitting on the floor with my cousin, Edwin, where they were taunting me, looking at me, talking about me, looking at me from the corner of their eyes, sneering at me. This was my first taste of my sister turning other family members against me. The learning process of this, thereafter, became continuous, but I couldn't see it at the time how much she hated me, resented me, as to why when all I ever wanted to do was love her. I had only one sister who came from my mother, which was my mother's first marriage, but I still called her my sister. But the sneering, the bullying, the intimidation and being told constantly I was worthless was ringing through my soul and had been for years, and played a massive part in planting my journey ahead, constructing my mannerisms and developing my character as I was programmed as a child as a horrible nasty little boy, worthless, skinny and small and unimportant.

As the weeks went by I entered my first Christmas in jail. I had to have a medical in which I was checked and weighed. To my shock I was giving my body weight at 9 stone 3 lb. I have never been 9 stone 3 lb. I didn't feel I was that skinny. I had grown a beard, my hair had grown. Bearing in mind I was thinning on top, I didn't realise how bad my condition was. The prison doctor said to me, the chaplain was doing photos for inmates to send home to their loved ones and if I wished to have a photo done, pop in and see him to send home a photo to my family. I said I would love to do that if that's possible, please book me in.

With this, right away I found the prison chaplain and asked if it was possible that I could have a photo done to send out to my mother. Within a day or two I had my photo taken. I waited a couple of weeks before I got the photo but when I did I couldn't believe what I was looking at - a thin, underweight man with a beard, with my hair growing at the sides and back, nothing on top. I never realised how bad I looked, and I never realised that I was then at the lowest point of my life, the most darkest, deepest point of my life. I didn't realise how low I had fallen and I didn't realise I was suffering from depression. I just got on with things, so I thought. I realised that prison had drained my heart and soul. Just by looking at that photo I realised how bad I was, but I wanted to send it home to my mother to show I am alive and I am well to the best of my ability. It was the only Christmas present I could send her, which could give her some hope that I was doing ok.

Christmas was a very lonely time. New Year's Eve was even harder and I could hear fireworks at the stroke of midnight, and my thoughts were of my mother, but at least my sister was there keeping her company, it was something at least. I used to sit regularly with Frankie and have a cup of tea in his cell and he would talk to me about his life, how he ended up there through a street fight where he stabbed man to death. Frankie stood about 6-ft 3, around 18 stone. He was a big man in his 40s approaching the near end of his sentence. I really liked Frank. He took me under his wing, showed me the prison way to pick your company, keep your head down and crack on. I found faith whilst in prison. It seemed to be, every time I was in a dark place the thought of Jesus, God the almighty made himself present to me.

I began to go to church every Sunday. It gave me a sense of peace, a sense of tranquillity, an element of forgiveness for the man I didn't want to be but had become. Faith got me through the darkest times of my life, all 9 stone 3 of me. Being in the church on a Sunday morning in prison gave me strength. For some reason, throughout my prison sentence so far, I always got to meet guys that had a bit of a reputation that was a big presence and was respected. They all seemed to take me under their wing. There must have been something they could see in me. I wasn't the usual Reebok Classic swinging shoulders type of inmate, I was just being me. I had no one to impress, there was no reason to be cocky, I was just being me.

Chapter 7

The Discovery of Me

The discovery of me began. Prison gave me discovery which gave me direction to the real me. I was beginning to learn. I was discovering so much about myself from a child growing up into adult life and into prison. I began to learn about myself and who and what I had become, and who I wanted to be.

Hours upon hours of writing about my life gave me insight into my life, on who I was as a person. I discovered the hate from my sister. I looked into her past from her father, from my mother's first marriage, in which her father was an alcoholic, an aggressive alcoholic who had been very present in my sister's upbringing in her early years. It was apparent this had affected her journey as a child and into her adult years which made her the person she was.

I clearly remember one occasion as a child. I said to my sister during one of her drunk and drugged rages that she was very much like her father, as what I used to hear from conversations of my mother of her ex-husband's heavy drinking when he would become aggressive and violent and loud, with a temper that matched.

This was my sister. She was programmed like the computer I am talking about; a young child's mind witnessing the drunken aggression which is programming the child's mind, a mind that was once pure and clear that knew of no injustice, no impurities, just curious. I looked at my situation with my sister and how she had been with me and the outcome in its strange twist was the same. Prior to prison I was using drugs on a regular occasion to escape reality. I became aggressive, I became impossible to live with, all my relationships were failures. I was too aggressive, punching doors, losing my temper - this was an outcome of bullying from my sister. The outcome of her father and his drunken rages was the outcome of my sister. The moral of this journey so far is the fact, if you bring your children up in an environment that is aggressive, that is fuelled with drugs and alcohol, with the bullying from either a brother or sister or mother or father - trust me, the damage to a child could be fatal in later years. As my sister was to me, as she was almost ten years older than me. Her actions were the same as her father and the actions of my sister became the actions of my aggressive ways too, a domino effect of life. Like she was programmed at an early age that stayed with her for the rest of her life.

As for me, I have discovered this, in its strange twisted way, this was my fate, this was my destiny and this was my journey of discovery through prison that actually helped me discover what I had become. I was not too late to put things right, find the 'who' I really am, and where I wanted to go with my life. Sadly, my sister never discovered this and still, to this day lives a very evil aggressive life, within herself still a selfish person that drinks and takes drugs. Maybe with age she may see some kind of light but I very much doubt that.

This new discovery of me was only going to aid my realisation, my new journey. It wasn't going to cure me, but at least I realised what had happened and why. From this moment in time during the first year of my prison sentence, I got my head down and knuckled down, kept myself to myself and picked my company very carefully. I did have a couple of scrapes with a couple of inmates but nothing that would have been any issue.

One occasion I witnessed whilst serving my sentence at HMP Coldingley was that there was a lifer that sadly took his life. He was in the opposite cell to me and one morning as all the doors unlocked, which are electronic at HMP Coldingley, - once the electronic system opened up all the doors that was your chance to empty your slop out pot in the toilets and make your way to the servery for your breakfast prior to going into your workplace – the body was discovered.

This was my first experience of seeing a prisoner commit suicide. When I brought my food back up to my cell I could see prison officers around the door of the cell opposite me. We were all confined to our cells for a little while. I then witnessed the inmate being brought out in a black zip up bag and carried out. This was tragic, sad, so sad, and horrific to see. Later it turned out he had been injecting heroin with a very old needle in between his toes and had been injecting everywhere with the same needle for such a long period of time. Rumour had it the heroin was far from clean and contained brick dust which had killed him. God rest his soul.

This vision has never left me, but gave me insight that prison will get you in the end. When you have no light at the end of your tunnel you look for ways of finding that light, whether to use drugs to overdose to end your life or any other means. It shows the desperate paths people will take to leave this world.

Yes, there was violence in prison on another occasion. A man was what they call "jugged" - this is where a jug is filled with boiling hot water from the boiler which is on the landing. Boiling hot water is mixed with sugar and the victim will receive the boiling hot water into the face where the sugar will stick. This I only witnessed once. The guy was what they call a "nonce" and was found out tipped off by the prison officers' "screws" to the cons. The scream was so intense I would imagine every block within that prison would have heard him. I've never seen anybody look in so much pain ever but for what he had done he deserved what he got, in my opinion, as the family of whatever child he abused will be suffering for the rest of their lives, including the child. The majority of these nonces, they only serve minimal sentences which made me so angry. Child abuse in any form is not acceptable, just not acceptable, sexual abuse is not acceptable and anyone that considers and thinks and acts on those thoughts deserves everything they get and hope every time he now looks in the mirror he has a reminder of what he had done and that will live with him in that mirror for the rest of his life too.

I ended up getting back into the gym in which as a prison gym you have limited equipment at limited times which was only on offer, but I wanted to get back in the gym. At 9 stone 3 lb I needed to look healthier when my mother would see me next. As the months proceeded I got in with guys in the kitchens, they would bring me out food for small tokens like phone cards etc.

I began to put some weight back on as I crept into a year and a half, almost 2 years into my sentence. I slowly began to put my weight back on, and thanks to my lovely, dear friend, Steve, for bringing my mother up again at Coldingley to see me, I needed to be stepping out for my visit looking healthier than last time. Despite all my inner feelings of darkness I thought I must look healthier for my mother and I put on at least a stone in weight. I was filling my clothes out again and I looked stronger in body and mind. I was very blessed with some beautiful people in my life. Steve, Paul and Tanya always wrote to me throughout my prison sentence, stood by my side; they did not leave me. I even got Paul to do a bodybuilding seminar at HMP Coldingley whilst he was in the height of his bodybuilding career. All 19 stone of him, at 5-ft 8, he looked great and would inspire the cons to hit the gym hard along with the best way to put on muscle with the diet we were given. These people never left my side. I will be eternally grateful for their loyalty and true appreciation.

The year 2000, The Millennium year, had been and gone. I dealt with it easier. I became stronger. I became healthier in mind and body. I was fighting fit, ready to take on the world outside. I still had a long way to go before parole but I did not focus on parole. I didn't want to build my hopes up and not get it and be let down and serve the full term of the sentence. So, I just knuckled down and got on with it. My new cellmate opposite me was Fowzi Badavi, an Arab Iranian; the only survivor of a 6-person group of democratic revolutionary front for the liberation of Arabistan that seized the Iranian embassy for six days in London in 1980. This was major national news in 1980 with scenes of the SAS climbing down the walls of the embassy. I remembered it being all over the national news, and that very terrorist was in the opposite cell to me. Fowzi was at the tail end of his sentence; he was the only survivor of the siege. He was sentenced for conspiracy to murder in 1981. I believe his release date was 2008.

I came across an absolute gentleman called Ronnie Field. Ronnie was Charlie Kray's co-defendant. I got chatting with Ronnie and told him about my case of which Ronnie truly understood the case of entrapment as we discovered whilst chatting that there was a strong possibility it was the same undercover police officers from New Scotland Yard. On further investigation Ronny told me to write to Charlie Kray which I did and weeks later I received a reply and I genuinely felt so sorry for Charlie.

Charlie received 12 years for plotting a drugs deal where undercover police officers had requested Charlie and Ronnie and another co-defendant to supply, which I believe was around approximately 39 million worth of cocaine in stages of drops, which was reported in the national papers, and which as normal, I would imagine extremely exaggerated. Myself and Charlie kept in touch, and further chats with Ronnie Field which all seemed very familiar, a very similar situation of entrapment and sounded very similar to the undercover police officers that were working within Scotland Yard - a unit, a very corrupt unit, that would incite people into manufactured crimes to get them off the streets. Sadly, Charlie Kray passed away whilst in prison like his brothers, all put behind bars because of their name. The tragic thing about all this is, there are people within the prison system that have done far worse crimes, actually committed serious offences and do far less time in prison. It's disgusting and one thing I did learn was corruption is on every level of life in the Government whom I call legal gangsters; they write their own rules and they break their own rules and they make their own rules to fit their own needs, legal villains, secret handshakes, freemasonry, backhanders of cash, say no more and this goes for the police also. Corruption within the police force on every level specifically within Scotland Yard was extremely high.

Sadly, all the Kray brothers passed away in prison. You have child molesters, "nonces", child rapists, woman beaters, horrible nasty vile creatures that end up with two years for sexually assaulting a child, absolutely disgusting, totally disgusting. Most of the government, in my opinion, are very strange people, and the high end of the police force equally of the same bent, bent, bent. And also, in some cases which I know to be true, well known villains acting secretly under code names as police informants with backhanders paying off the old bill so they can work their operations quietly. They call this "The underworld". That's a world I wish not to be part of.

As the years passed into my sentence, I grew stronger, preparing myself to apply for parole but once again another surprising knock came at my cell door. I received a letter from Tallahassee, Florida. An extremely strange letter, as in my thoughts I knew of nobody in Tallahassee. I had never even heard of the place before. I come from Chatham. The closest I'd been to being abroad was Leysdown. This letter I proceeded to read on, that a Mr Claude Dubok had been arrested for bribing a United States federal judge and been arrested for money laundering and two undercover police officers had been arrested on suspicion of corruption. I proceeded to read that these two undercover police officers were subsequently the two undercover police officers that were involved in the investigation of me. Now this was surprising, it was what I needed to read. Albeit I was shocked, and needed to read this letter a number of times to understand what it was saying.

When I read it, I thought it was indicating that I was party to this money laundering charge and bribing a United States federal judge, but thankfully I read it properly and it was the investigation into two undercover police officers working out of New Scotland Yard and they both were under investigation by the FBI and the legal team of Claud Dubok. The letter proceeded to then read on that the attorney of Claude Dubok wished to visit me in the United Kingdom supported by a retired FBI agent working with the legal team's attorney.

Now this couldn't have come at any worse time as I approached to apply for my parole. It just seemed my name even after being sentenced is still being thrown around outside, even being mentioned in a court in Tallahassee, Florida. The two undercover police officers had acted for New Scotland Yard. They obviously were truly of a corrupt nature and were under investigation for the way they had been working. I spoke to Ronnie Field about this and even he said all this sounded very much like the two undercover police officers that were party to their case. That very night I drafted a letter to be sent, and I sent my version of events in a letter with descriptions of the two undercover police officers that had me under investigation and party to the armed robbery of the nightclub. Having a retired FBI agent visit me in prison was somewhat strange. I mean the FBI really, but it goes to show the level of corruption within New Scotland Yard. George and Paul were obviously pseudonyms to cover their real identity. I hope they got their justice as it very much sounded like they were under investigation for their own wrongdoings in setting people up, and villains working with them, like Eddie, who set me up so they could carry on with their own crimes with most likely backhanders to the police.

I placed my parole application in with anticipation. I truly wanted to get home to my mother. After three years in prison I was now offered a 'D' category prison after completing various offending behaviour courses which I had to do, which would aid me with better prospects of getting my parole. I completed all the courses as requested. I was offered HMP Spring Hill in Buckingham and this was a delight and music to my ears as this was an open prison where I could obtain town visits and even the opportunities to get back into society with working within the community. The news had come, I had been granted parole.

With this happy news I telephoned my mother as I did on various occasions when I had a phone card. I told my mother I had been granted parole, she cried with pure joy. My release date was due 2002. The thought of having a release date was strange but beautiful, and I thought I'd been given the chance to go to an open prison and the chance to feel a little freedom for a crime that didn't even happen which cost the tax payer thousands upon thousands of pounds for nothing.

I planned for a visit for Steve to bring my mother up to HMP Springhill in Buckingham. I was given my transfer date to Springhill. The day finally came for my transfer with the usual routine of handcuffs placed in a sweat box and awaited my transfer from HMP Coldingley to HMP Springhill where I would finish off the remainder of my sentence with a little bit of freedom. Whilst travelling in the prison van, once again the realisation of freedom was getting close. Looking out of the prison window, life looked so beautiful, seeing the flowers and people walking, cars driving, everything looked modern – strange, how life had moved on so much in just under three years, how much life had changed, even CD players had come in and tapes were gone during my time in prison. DVD players, never seen the likes of these. So many changes in such a short space of time.

As the prison van drove into the gates of HMP Springhill I could see no wall, no barbed wire. In fact, there was nothing stopping any prisoner from walking out. It looked so free, so open, so clear. Prison had never looked so beautiful. As I was walked off the prison van into reception with my HMP bag with my clothes I was then shown the induction hut where I had to share a room. I couldn't call it a cell because there was no lock on the door, there was no slamming of a steel door. It was a wooden door like a normal wooden door of a normal home with a room with two beds like a normal bedroom, and your own key to the door - completely different to what I'd been used to for almost three years. I was sharing a room with a guy called Pops. Pops was Jamaican, in his 60s, serving time for drug smuggling. I absolutely loved this guy straight away, a true character. I was never in favour of sharing a room with anybody but Pops was absolutely a delight. I loved him. Pops Carrington we called him.

With any new prison the first thing was getting settled and upon association I had my first chance to walk around the prison. There was a great big field with trees all around the edges. A tune came into my mind by The Who – 'I can see for miles and miles' - that tune was a beautiful reminder of freedom because I could actually see for miles and miles. For almost three years I had been looking at a concrete wall just meters in front of me, with barbed wire, security cameras, but now I was looking at trees and I could actually see for miles and miles. I played that tune in my head for weeks. I felt revitalised, I felt I'd been given a second chance of life, and within a week or two my lovely friend, Steve, once again popped in with my mother to see me. Paul and Tanya, my dear friends, had also booked in to see me.

Eventually I was moved to another hut called 'N' hut. I was given another room mate called Jason, a very stocky guy; wasn't sure about him at first but as time went on he was an absolute diamond. We got on so well, a true diamond of life. I got to know various people whilst at HMP Springhill. Martin was absolute superstar ex armed robber, we totally clicked straight away. Opposite to me was a guy called Russell Tate. His brother was shot in a Range Rover in Essex. It was a very notorious case of three men shot in their Range Rover. Pat Tate was his brother that had been one of the men shot. I really liked Russell.

Russell had told me the story about his brother and it was actually quite heart-breaking when Russel explained to me that a film was due out about the shootings.

I thought about this quite deeply, how hard must it be to watch films about your loved ones being shot, specially, when you've got no say in the matter. I think that's wrong. At the end of the day these people have mothers and fathers, and brothers or sisters. It must be hard for the families especially for mothers, bearing in mind how close I am to my mother, she is my world and I would hate to think she would watch a film about her son being shot. We all got on really well with Russell, Martin, Jason and Alfie. But there was one chap called Dene Lingham. Now, I just adored this guy, we laughed and laughed. We had this thing called the calling where I would hear his call and I would run to him for a cuddle. I loved the man. It's crazy how such strong bonds are made with certain people which just makes life in such hard times so much more bearable. And, of course, another good guy that was with me at Coldingley was Darren Soper, another true solid soul. I also became very close friends with a guy called Brian Long - another former armed robber serving 12 years. This guy was just amazing. We clicked like family. True old school values.

Life was getting better, I was now tipping the scales at 15 stone. I had been working out in the gym regularly, training hard, eating loads. I was strong in heart and soul, and was preparing for life on the outside. My parole was granted and I was blessed, truly blessed, finally light at the end of a very dark cold tunnel. We had town visits where we could go out into society and mingle with human life, something I hadn't done for almost three years, but I loved it. Paul and Tanya came to visit me at HMP Springhill. Their loyalty as friends was so true, they both kept in touch throughout my sentence and wrote regularly. I was truly blessed.

As these were town visits, your visitors could pick you up and take you out for the day. Paul had a stunning car, a Subaru P1. This car looked amazing and it was a treat for me to be in a car, let alone something as pretty as that. I had been walking in a circle for over three years in prison exercise yard, now I'm in a car which felt strange, but it was lovely to feel alive and free once more. Paul took me down through the lanes and opened up on the speed, I held on for life. I had been walking pace for over three years and now I am hundred miles an hour. Tanya sat in the back of the car so relaxed. I was in pure fear of the speed but it was a happy memory made, that will never ever leave me.

One day whilst working on farms and gardens a prison officer came to talk to me. He said the magic words, "Clive, you can go home today." I had a three-weeks' trial in which I was told I had to surrender into custody every time I entered the court. Whilst on bail these were included in days off your sentence. I thought I would apply for these days back. With God's blessings I was granted the three weeks court days off my sentence which took me to Christmas 2002. What a surprise, what a shock I'm going home, I'm finally going home! I never told my mother, I didn't call her, I didn't let her know, I wanted to surprise her.

As I was clearing my belongings from my room on the resettlement unit a tune came on the radio. Songs always have a relevant part in time and emotion for that moment, and this tune was by Kate Bush, 'Running Up That Hill'. This song fitted that moment in time, the words fitted that moment, "Do you want to feel how it feels, do you want to know, know how it doesn't hurt me, do you want to hear about the deal that I'm making, I'd make a deal with God and I'd get him to swap our places, be running up that road, he's running up that hill be running up that building." It was time to go home I had done my time. I'm coming home.

⚫

Chapter 8

Freedom to an Uncertain Path

D estination home. Three and a half years had passed, and home is on the horizon. I had only seen my mother four times in three and a half years. Knowing the damage that I did, knowing the feelings that I had left my mother with, knowing that she suffered as a result of my prison sentence is something that will haunt me for the rest of my eternal life.

The anticipation that was within me was deep, very deep, but deep within my heart and soul I've been waiting for a long time to be back home with my mother. The path that I had taken was one of destruction not only to myself but to the ones I love. Knowing I left my mother to pay for a funeral she couldn't afford and a headstone which still wasn't present on my father's grave. The thoughts I had run through my mind and had not left me from the day I entered prison, tears ran down my face. Finally, destination home.

As I approached the door of my mother's home I knocked on the door. I didn't tell my mother that I had received my court days back. This was a complete surprise for me to be home. I knocked on the door. I could hear my mother's footsteps as she approached the door, my mother then opened the door and there I stood. "I'm home, Mum," I said. The look on my mother's face was pure joy. My mother then proceeded to say, "You haven't escaped, have you?" I laughed and said, "You're safe." I gave my mother a massive cuddle, a reassuring cuddle, it felt very spiritual, very real, very true, all those thoughts in my head of prison were still very apparent but I was home with my mother, the moment I'd been waiting for, for so long.

Walking into the flat was a strange feeling, very hard, a feeling I will never forget. It was as if I'd never left, as if three and a half years never happened but of course it had and a lot of damage was done in between which was completely my doing, nobody else's, just my doing.

This was a fresh page and new chapter and I had to get it right this time. I remember sitting down as my mother made me a cup of tea. I remembered looking around thinking to myself it was as if nothing had changed. I blinked and three and a half years had passed and I was back. I was unsure about the feeling. It didn't make sense, but the blessing was, I was home, and home is where the heart is.

As I said, this feeling was truly very strange. It was as if I was waiting to be told when my dinner was, the schedule of prison and the daily routine of jail was gone. I should be feeling elated, happy, that I was happy to be home but it just felt very strange.

I proceeded to tell my mother that I would be on licence until the end of the seven-year sentence and that I would be on probation for a period of time until they deemed me fit enough to become a normal member of the public. My mind was running wild with plans of where I was going to live. The address for my licence was my mother's address at which my mother said I could stay for as long as I needed. It was a lovely evening, one that I would remember for the rest of my life because of the strange feeling that I had, when you've waited for something so long and you finally receive it. Whatever that may be, the feeling of that, is one that stays with you. All those nights worrying, the fear, the anticipation, the stress, the depression, the weight loss, pretending to be ok, battling demons within your mind, face the fears you never thought you'd face and being around people you didn't want to be around was all a distant memory but still so real.

Very mixed emotions, but I had happiness deep within my heart. I loved being back in the arms of my mother, the beautiful soul that I felt went to the ends of the earth to put food on the table. We chatted away that evening as if nothing had happened. I could see my mother was happy to have me home and her little cat that she introduced me to as Tigger. She was cute. That very night I slept on the sofa. It was so strange. All of a sudden, my routines had all changed. There was no role check, there was no being told what to do and when to do it, it was all new all over again. I hardly slept that night.

I had to attend probation the following day and set out a plan to obtain unemployment benefits to get me back into society with a view to obtain full-time employment which was my goal, so I could find a little flat for myself to live in. Getting back into day-to-day life was extremely difficult after being told what to do for so long. Even though I was introduced to the outside world by the occasional town visit, you are still told what to do and when to do it; you become institutionalized.

But I didn't recognise that at that moment in time I just needed to get back into normal society, find a job, find a flat and try and fit in again in a world I'd not been around for three and a half years. I got back in contact with Brian who had been released prior to me after serving twelve years for armed robbery. We met in London at a pub called the Prospect of Whitney, a lovely pub situated on the River Thames. We met for a drink and a chat just to see how life was going for him after serving twelve years. It was hard enough for me to serve three and a half years of a seven-year sentence let alone serving twelve years. So much had changed in such a short space of time, twelve years is over a decade. Brian was an old school villain, I loved him. Brian was very close friends with Charlie Kray and various other known faces. Brian was a very successful businessman during the 80s in more ways than one.

If you have ever seen the film 'The Long Good Friday' there is a part within that film where Bob Hoskins stands on the tail end of a boat and says, "There's been peace for ten years, now there's going to be an eruption," or words to that effect. It just fitted that moment for me as to where I was actually going to go in life. From the moment you leave prison you have a moment where you think you have made heaps of very useful contacts whilst in prison from drug dealers to armed robbers - a wealth of contacts where you could go if you so wished to make a huge amount of money in a bad way.

But I wanted to go on the straight and narrow. I didn't wish to revert back to heavy crime or face the loss of freedom again and the next sentence would be double figures without a doubt and knowing the feelings I had how corrupt the police force truly are, if they want you off the streets they will get you off the streets, there's no ifs, no buts, you do not stand a chance.

Meeting Brian was fantastic and we became extremely close friends. Yes, I'm not going to deny we've made a few quid by bending the rules slightly but they were only slightly, nothing that would have put me in prison, just a little fun. But my goal was to find full-time employment. That was my ambition. It was a must. I needed to get my life back on track but I saw a lot of obstacles ahead. My probation officer explained to me what I needed to do to find employment and I proceeded to attend the local Jobcentre to apply for jobs. I sent off a number of applications and I was advised by my probation officer I must put down on all my paperwork, on any application forms, that I had served a prison sentence. When I left prison, I had to sign a document which is called The Firearms Act.

I sent quite a few applications for employment and the majority never replied. I attended job interview upon job interview and no one took the time to reply back to me. I must have attended at least twenty or more job interviews within a space of two months and none of them gave me a chance. It was a nightmare. I was on licence. I was on probation. I was told in every job interview that I went for in my situation, the usual words, "I will get back to you," and very rarely they did reply. But when they did it was a 'no'.

I was beginning to get very disheartened with society that they would not give me a chance, nobody would come near me, nobody would employ me, it was a nightmare. I was slowly slipping back into my old self. I began using cocaine. I was drinking and clubbing regularly with various friends that I had met whilst out with Brian. The cocaine was becoming regular. I didn't realize it was hiding a multitude of emotions that had not been dealt with. It was my escape from reality, slipping back into the ways I was, prior to going into prison. I met up with my sister. There was no love there, but I had to keep a face for my mother. She was still using drugs and she was still drinking. There was absolutely no change there, whatsoever. She was still the same sister I had left prior to going into prison.

Things weren't good. In fact, they were terrible. I managed to move into a studio bedsit and within this bedsit there was a small sofa bed and a TV and a very small kitchen with a shower and toilet. It was almost the size of a prison cell, so it felt. But it was home, so I thought. I saw my mother daily and one particular day I took her to my father's grave. I had been putting it off for some time as the guilt within me was strong and the promise I had made to my father was still very deep within my heart that I had let him down drastically, but I had to take my mother up to see my father's grave. It was something I had to do. On the approach to walking up to his grave I could see his little wooden cross which was the same wooden cross that was there many years before. My mother had finally paid all of the funeral costs at £15 per week for years, from washing up the dishes in a local café. She had struggled to pay for the funeral for all those years whilst I was in prison, and that broke my heart, it truly did.

Whilst looking at my father's cross I said to myself that I was so sorry. I felt so sorry that I had let him down but one thing I did promise - to correct my wrongs and make amends for the damage that I'd done. I blew a kiss to my father's cross and walked my mother back to the car. She hardly talked as it was hard for her to stand by her husband's grave and look at a wooden cross that was crumbling.

Life was getting harder. This was not what I imagined it to be after being released from prison. This was not like I had anticipated it to be, at all. One particular evening, whilst I sat in my studio bedsit, I sat and listened to the silence. I can remember this as if it was yesterday. The feeling that came upon me was dark, truly dark. I listened to more of the silence and the realization how much I missed prison. I truly missed prison. I missed the routine, I missed my friends, I missed having a laugh. There was no stress, there was no worry, there was nothing other than routine. I absolutely loved prison. The isolation suited me. I didn't have to worry about paying for electric light bills, I didn't have to worry about paying the rent, I didn't have to worry about anything other than breakfast, lunch and dinner and bang up that was it. I missed that routine.

But I remember sitting, listening to the silence and I was in such a dark place. I wanted to end my life. Looking back at my life, it had been shambles, being bullied, intimidated, sexually assaulted, child abuse, all instigated by my sister - she had made my life hell. All these thoughts were running through my head, my mind was running wild with crazy emotions, the cold deep darkness of my soul. It was black, truly black. I had realised I was back in the big, wide world and I didn't like it. I didn't like where I was and I didn't want to be here anymore feeling this way. This was the first time I contemplated suicide and I really meant it. I cried and cried and cried. I wanted to go back to prison. It was my home. I had waited for three and a half years for silence and stress and worry, I hadn't moved on. I had just stepped right back into where I was, again, only this time I was much more damaged. I had become institutionalized within that three-and-a-half-year period. I realised that there was no real help for prisoners on release, you get your probation, you keep your head down, finish your licence and you're out, you're good, you're done. But there I was contemplating taking my life.

Everybody would be better off without me if I were gone, would I be better off not here? I remember crying so much that I was ready to go. I decided to take heaps of tablets of a mixture of everything from cocaine to MDMA. I thought, was it the paranoia again that was getting to me? I started using Ecstasy when I was clubbing with my friends. I was in the darkest place I could have ever been. I had waited three and a half years for this silence. The uncertainty of life.

When someone contemplates suicide it's how you're going to do it. Heaps of drugs and tablets to fall asleep and to slowly die? Jumping off a bridge was not an option for me but the thought of suicide was strong. I didn't realise I was suffering from severe depression. I would go clubbing regularly at our local night club with my friends and I would be taking heaps of ecstasy tablets to feel happy. Everyone thought I was having a good time dancing away but what I was actually doing was escaping reality taking myself away from it all. When all the drugs wore off and I suffered the horrid come down for the week, that was when reality would come back again, and before the weekend was here I would be back on the drugs again, cocaine, MDMA and Ecstasy. I would swallow two to three tablets of Ecstasy in one go. My body got so used to them, in the end I needed a lot for it to work again. This became a regular occurrence. That very night I was quite happy to swallow heaps of Ecstasy and just die.

That night I fell asleep and woke up to a new day. The thoughts of suicide were still running through my mind. I had messed everybody's life up. Every relationship I had ever had was a failure, I was bad tempered and aggressive. When I looked deep into my life I realised I was becoming my sister - nasty, horrible, aggressive, evil creature. I did not want to become that person because I knew how much damage that person did to me. I did not want to do that to other people.

I was not in a good place for a long time. I was back on steroids again and training. I started training with a lovely guy called Paul Fryer. He was an absolute true gent. We became very close friends and training partners. He used to work at a nightclub called The Avenue.

Paul called me and told me of a girl working at the club that knew me many years ago. This girl explained to Paul how bad I used to be many years ago, and I had to admit I wasn't a nice person. I had never been violent towards any woman, I would smash doors, punch holes in doors, punch windscreens of cars. I'd been doing this since the age of seven years from the point of abuse and intimidation and bullying from my sister. It was never the steroids that created this animal, it was the damage that had been done internally to my mind and the steroids promoted that side of me more. Paul explained that the girl at the club wished to talk to me regarding a little girl that was to be my daughter, with a view to put things right.

For years I believed I never had a daughter. I had closed that door shut. A meeting was arranged. The meeting with me and the girl from the club. Years had passed and so much was said when we ended our relationship, and for years I strongly believed I never had a daughter. I was showed a photo of this little girl and I knew she was mine. I could see the strong resemblance of me in her. She was eleven years old. This was what I needed to get straight again. I was given my purpose to rebuild a bond between us and one that I would love and cherish. My last vision of my daughter was on my father's knee, smiling. Hours later my father died and within weeks I lost a daughter too when I was told she was not my child. I lost three people when my father died. I lost my father and a sister the day she was drunk and told me the day of my father's funeral she never loved me as a brother. Weeks later I was told I never had a daughter. No wonder I went off the rails and lost my way. Everything I learn to love leaves me or betrays me. Love was a word I failed to understand.

Sadly, my drug usage was not slowing down weekend after weekend after weekend of approximately two years. I was taking cocaine, MDMA and Ecstasy mixed with Speed. All my friends at that time thought I was such a bundle of fun, always dancing at the club every weekend. I came across so happy. I just wanted to make up for the lost years, but underneath all the drug usage I was suffering, I was suffering so badly. Some nights after leaving the club I would walk to a cemetery at the end of our road and fall asleep lying on one particular grave. I did this every time, every weekend and I would normally receive a call from one of the doormen from the club, one of the guys that used to visit me with Paul. His name was Steve McNeil. He would call me and pick me up from the cemetery and take me back home. I didn't realise I was suffering from depression. I never realised about depression. Depression was never really talked about, it wasn't in the highlight, it wasn't ever mentioned. Men were men, sort yourself out and man up was the attitude. I carried that attitude and lived with that motto. But I was a broken man in more ways than one. I was suffering so badly I just didn't realise how bad I actually was. That depression got worse and the drug usage was becoming more regular. All the friends that I had around me encouraged me. It wasn't anything of their wrongdoing. They just thought I was having fun but I was in a bad way. I had no purpose, no reason, no motivation to find a job when every conceivable job I went for, I got turned down. As soon as I told them I was in prison they didn't want to know more. There was one job that I went for. I told them nothing about my criminal record. It was an industrial door company. I really liked the owners of the business.

The position was for an engineer's mate. The interview was amazing and the owner of the company said, can I start Monday? I was shocked and overwhelmed with excitement. For once I had been given a chance. I finally had a legitimate job. I was still using drugs every weekend to mask my feelings to get me through the week of work and life. I loved my job. However now that I was earning I could buy more drugs. Deep down the fight against myself was, that I wanted to make a better life for my mother and my daughter, to try and put everything back in place, but I was still struggling. I had met a girl, we had a relationship for a number of weeks, however that failed and she decided to go to my employer and tell them that I had been in prison and she proceeded to tell them it was an armed robbery.

As I went into work the next morning I was taken into the office and told I was no longer needed for employment as I had not declared that I had been in prison, and due to fitting industrial doors and security doors it was not of a suitable nature for a person of my past record to be in such an employment. I was heartbroken. I was then told that when my van was searched they found syringes which I was using for steroids. I felt ashamed of myself.

Things did not look good once again. Women were very unkind to me. Was it justified sometimes when I would punch a hole in the door, when I would lose my head? Yes, I deserved what I got at times. But was it justified to tell my employer that I served a prison sentence? 'No' is the answer to that, that was evil.

When I lost my temper and would shout, all I could see at times was visions of my sister, the way she treated me. I never trusted women. I didn't put my love into women. I was too scared to love them in case they did further damage to my mind. Every woman I ever met, I was paranoid about, if they were seeing someone else. I believed they were lying to me all the time as my experience with the female species was not of a good nature and this was an implant from seven years old, from the damage my sister did to me.

I was beginning to have a lot of nightmares about prison, old dark Victorian prisons, doors slamming, keys rattling, these nightmares were very frequent and they were getting worse over a period of time, but once again I just thought they were dreams, nothing to be concerned about, nothing to worry about, just nightmares. We all have them, they come and they go, but nevertheless there were nightmares, the flashbacks and the echoes of inmates, jail doors slamming.

Life wasn't very pretty. In fact, it was very dark. I was losing my way once again. The drugs were getting the better of me and doing me a tremendous amount of damage emotionally.

I couldn't cope any longer. The thoughts of suicide were coming back again, but they were just thoughts. I looked at the mess of my life, the damage I had done to my mother, and the people that I thought loved me had done nothing but damage me.

I started seeing my daughter on a regular basis. Most weekends we would meet up and I would take her out for the day. I looked forward to these days, they gave me a smile. I could tell my daughter found it hard to come to terms that she had a father. It was all new for us both. It was strange but I wanted to show love and not show the tragic side of me which has had a knock-on effect through my whole family. I did not wish to subject my daughter to that.

I fancied a nice car. I'd been driving around in bangers, heaps, some cars never had MOTs or tax and I never had any insurance. But I fancied a nice car. I found a magazine called the Auto Trader and found myself a nice car. A nice Mercedes and decided to steal it. I telephoned the owner to meet in a selected meeting place where I would steal the car. I met the guys just off a country lane and took it for a test drive with them in the car. As they got out of the car I drove it off. I could see them in my rear-view mirror looking bewildered but I didn't care, I just needed a nice car to drive. I found another car in a different area and copied the number plates and had a set of number plates made which I put on the stolen car I was driving.

I drove this car around for about four months and decided to sell it as a ringer. I was not in a good place but I had to make a change. There was something inside of me, the real me. There was a good person within me. I didn't want to be this aggressive steroid taking drug addict because it was the path that was shown to me as a child when I would see my sister drinking heavily, taking drugs, cocaine, heroin, witnessing everything as a child, growing up, and now I was walking that path too.

I had witnessed my sister following the footsteps of her father, my mother's first husband. He was a continuous heavy drinker and alcoholic. She had witnessed her father as an alcoholic, as a violent alcoholic which she then was programmed to be from childhood. She then passed that on to me as a child and I was living that person. What you witness as a child, growing up, leaves a mark on a child's mind. A child's mind is the computer, the eyes give the brain the information. The child is being programmed to become a character of life, to become a person, to become a teenager, to become an adult. What you see as a child is your journey, your path, it becomes your destiny.

I wanted to join the Royal Navy as a child. I wanted to make my parents proud of me. My father said the Royal Navy was something I shouldn't be looking at. I took his advice and I never applied. It was my dream. I wanted to feel proud of myself as a human, as a person but I decided it obviously wasn't meant to be.

The continuation of dreams of prison were very present. I was a lost soul with no direction. From leaving prison, there was no help, there was no reform, probation wasn't bothered I couldn't find a job. I could not find employment or anybody that would take me on due to my prison record. Especially within the local community people knew of the murder charge, the accusations of shooting people, armed robbery, car theft, drug dealing - what chance did I stand?

The drug abuse got worse, the comedowns got worse, the darkness got worse, watching my mother struggle financially got worse. The hate for my sister for what she had done to me as a child got worse, the regrets got worse, everything came to a head.

One particular night whilst clubbing I decided to drop four Ecstasy tablets at once. This was how bad I was and the friends I was clubbing with at the time just thought it was fun, but they didn't know I'd taken four Ecstasy tablets. That very night was the turning point of my life. I started to shiver, I felt cold. Shivering, I ran to the toilet of the nightclub and put my fingers down my throat to try and bring up the Ecstasy tablets I had swallowed. I was really sick. I remember my head was spinning, echoing voices, everything was spinning, the voices. My mind was telling me to get up. Something within me was telling me to stand up. I was pouring with sweat. I managed to get up and proceeded to leave the club to find a taxi to go home. I thought this was the end and I was going to die. The drugs, everything I took, got hold of me but this was the turning point. I didn't actually want to die. Even though I took more and more drugs to die, I didn't care anymore but when it came to facing death I was afraid. But I actually wanted to go because I didn't fulfil the promise I had made to my father. The battle of emotions of fight or flight.

I managed to get home safely. I left my friends behind at the club. My phone had a number of messages and missed calls from them wondering where I was. I got home and wrote a note to say goodbye to everybody as I strongly believed I was going to die. I felt that rough. I left a note on the bedside table so if I didn't wake in the morning I had my farewells in a letter.

The morning had come and I opened my eyes to life. I realised what I had done. I realised how bad I had been. My eyes opened to life. I was alive. I looked at the letter I had left on the bedside table. I screwed it up and threw it in the bin. That was the very last time I was ever going to take drugs. This was a wake-up call, one that nearly took my life. Ecstasy nearly killed me, the drugs nearly killed me. I was killing myself slowly and losing a grip, blaming myself for the life I had been given. Things had to change. I had to pull away from the friends that I had around me. It wasn't their fault. They were just taking drugs to have a good evening, they were not using drugs to the levels that I was. They never realised how much I was taking and the reasons why I was taking so much drugs. I had become an addict. This was the point of change. I had to do something to fight for, to stay alive and to fulfil the promise I had made to my father, not letting my past break my journey ahead which it was doing dramatically. This was my turning point. Something within me, whatever that was, was fighting hard; my heart and soul wanted out from this dark place. I had to make changes or I would either die or end up back behind bars.

Chapter 9

I'm Just a Soul whose Intentions are Good

'Don't Let Me Be Misunderstood. Baby, can you understand me now? Sometimes I get mad, don't you know, no one alive can always be an angel? When things go wrong, I seem to go bad. I'm just a soul whose intentions are good. Oh Lord, don't let me be misunderstood.'

Listening to this tune as I drove down a very narrow country lane, the lyrics to this tune fitted the feelings within my soul. The words to this song were my life. It felt as if it was written for me. 'Yeah, baby sometimes I'm so carefree, with joy that's hard to hide, Yeah, and other times it seems all I have is worry, and then you see my other side.'

This particular moment in time, everything about it, the country lane, the summer sun, nature. A moment of cleansing, turning a page of life as you flick through the chapters in your mind, self-analysis, self-assessment. The realisation of what I had become, who I didn't want to be, what had become of me, this was not the real me. I had to lay Clive Sands to rest. The name was cursed, the surname Sands was my father's surname which I loved and respected. But the name Clive I never liked. In fact, I hated it. It was my sister that named me Clive and for that reason alone Clive had to be laid to rest. I didn't like what Clive had become and the journey ahead for Clive was not right in any way, shape or form.

Listening to this tune, was a turning point of my life. It was as if it was meant to be, as if it was meant to happen. The Lord was giving me a sign. I was on the road to absolute destruction to the point it was going to kill me. I'd given my mother enough heartache over the years due to the damage that had been done to me through people that I loved; it had to all end.

This was a point of change not just from direction but my name. I was always a massive fan of the Rocky films. A man that came from absolutely nowhere, a story of a survivor of life if, from the Bronx of the dirty streets of Philadelphia, an unknown man creates his destiny. The film Rocky was a massive inspiration to me as a child. The inspiration of Rocky was something I modelled myself on, as a good soul that was struggling with life. I decided to change my name and for it to be Rocky. The plan was to legally change my name by deed poll. I needed a clean slate of life for a new destination, a fresh chapter and new page - all be it sounds so crazy but it made so much sense I needed to feel psychologically cleansed from Clive Sands. I hated him and what he was about to become for the rest of his life. He had to be laid to rest and now was the time. "Oh lord, Please Don't Let Me Be Misunderstood."

Within this new chapter of Rocky there had to be new changes, new directions and I had to create a life ahead of me of the person I wanted to be, not what I had become. I knew this was the right thing to do. It felt completely right. I didn't care what people thought of me, how crazy this sounded, it felt good for me. It was me that had to do the right thing for myself. For once in my life, if I didn't make the changes right now I was going to end up destroying everything and everybody else in my life around me. Just like my sister did to me and just like her father did to her it was going to happen to me too, and the domino effect of this was going to be never ending heartache. I had my daughter in my life, I could not let my past journey, my past destination of pure destruction infect her life or anybody else's life that would have been close to me. Time for change. I proceeded to seek a solicitor with the prospect of changing my name and all my legal documentation surrounding it. Driving licence, passport, bank details, everything.

A solicitor drafted a legal document which I was going to produce for all my documents to be changed. I was now Rocky Amore. The reason why I chose the surname Amore was, it was Italian for love. For many reasons I chose Amore because love was a massive part of my life I didn't understand. Love had failed me in many ways, the way I treated people, specifically relationships that I failed in due to the fact I didn't trust any woman that I was dating or in a relationship with. I didn't understand love. I feared love to the point I would destroy any love. Rocky Amore was born in a new fresh chapter of life. I was going to change my destination and leave Clive Sands in the past and lay him to rest.

People I know must have thought I was mad. People must have thought he is back taking too many drugs again, but that particular night when I overdosed on Ecstasy, that was the turning point that I was never going to use drugs ever again. The fear that that it gave me with even writing a note to my loved ones specifically my mother to say goodbye, and for her to find her son dead would have destroyed my mother. After losing her husband at 54 years old, she would have also lost her son. My mother was still a young woman that lost the love of her life. She had lost her soulmate, she had lost the most beautiful gift. Her soul was lost without my father and for her to find her son dead and for her to attend my funeral due to my selfish attitude to life, this would have only proved one thing - that I failed the love for my mother, and the promise I made to my father would have clearly been broken.

Rocky Amore, I'm here now. No more drugs, no more partying, move on. New chapter, I have a second chance at life and behold the most beautiful gift that we are blessed with, the appreciation to our mothers and fathers that created us and placed us on this earth. It's down to our mothers and fathers for our life and to disrespect that gift is absolutely tragic.

With this new journey ahead, I had started to seek legitimate employment. I felt a totally different man. It was difficult for my friends to suddenly change from calling me Clive to Rocky. In fact, in some cases it was so funny when people would slip from "Clive" to "ok sorry Rocky". It was hilarious but my friends, my beautiful friends, God bless their souls, they made me smile. They accepted the new me, they accepted the new Rocky and everyone called me Rocky to Rocks for short.

I made more effort with my mother. I made regular visits to pick up my daughter every single weekend. My objective was to include her in my life in every day, every minute, every second to show her real, true love, to include her in everything I did and open up the arms to the beautiful world that surrounds us and get rid of the negativity that would pull us into the depths of the demon's soul where he would keep you, and he would eat your soul, drain your heart of all its energy and destroy you and smile at you at the same time. This demon was my sister.

It was very difficult for me to keep the peace. My sister was unfortunately in my life. I wanted to completely shut the door on her but I know that would have hurt my mother. I could not do that to her. My mother wouldn't have wanted that, but I planned within my mind and it was a thought that was going to stay with me. God forbid the day I would lose my mother, the door on my sister would be firmly shut for eternal life as the damage she had done to me, the abuse that I received from the age of seven years, will be finally laid to rest that day my mother would be with my father again. But in the meantime, for the sake of my mother I would keep the peace.

I was training at a little local gym. I distanced myself from everyone else for a little while to seek new avenues and new friends with a view to a new destination. Over a period of weeks, I became very close friends with a young lad called Jake. He had a cracking physique for a young lad with great potential to be a fantastic bodybuilder. We clicked straight away and became training partners. I then became very close friends with his father, Ray. Ray owned a tarmacking company which was a local business that worked directly for the council as well as private work roads and driveways.

After a period of weeks, we became very good friends. On one particular training day Ray asked me what I was doing for work. I explained I had been doing a little bit of labouring here and there but nothing substantial and nothing permanent. He then asked me if I would be interested in some labouring work and if my licence was suitable to drive a HGV 7 ton lorry. I had passed my driving test in

1987 and my driving licence was suitable enough to drive a 7-tonne lorry. Ray asked me if I fancied starting work the following Monday morning on day money with the prospect of earning price work money. I jumped at the chance of this new opportunity.

The feeling of having a full-time job earning a regular wage gave me a great energy. This was the opportunity I absolutely needed. It just so felt since I changed my name it was as if everything was clicking into place. The jigsaw puzzle of my life was being placed piece by piece correctly. This new job was my new page and exactly what I needed.

I told my mother I had a new job and she was so pleased to hear her son finally had taken steps forwards rather than backwards with life and fulfilled a journey of Rocky and become a better person. Learned to love, learned to give people the time of my day, to be kind and rid the aggression that was making my life hell. I needed to rid the aggressive demon. I hated him. It was not me that was misunderstood but it was the person that I had become. Everything was falling into place. Ray bought me a little van for work and I started earning regular money. I would give my mother money weekly to help with day to day life like food shopping. I managed to save a little bit of money over a period of weeks and I started looking for a little flat for myself. I was flicking through the local paper and came across a beautiful riverside apartment which had not been built yet but was for rental very soon. I thought to myself: would I really stand a chance of something so beautiful? To live right on the River Medway, in a riverside apartment? But I was a believer in life that if you never ask you don't get. I contacted the letting agent dealing regarding the flat with a view to make an appointment.

On the day of the appointment I made sure I finished work a little earlier with permission from Ray as I explained to him I had an appointment with the letting agent regarding a flat which was on St Mary's Island in Chatham. I had enough money for a deposit which I had saved. I loved my new job, myself, and Jake was part of a two-man gang tarmacking pot holes and footpath patching. It was easy work and I was earning money and I felt alive.

I attended the appointment with the letting agent and behind the counter was a very pleasant brunette lady mid 30s. A truly lovely lady. I gave all my details, she showed me the brochure regarding the apartment and how it would look once it had been built. We were talking several months away before completion but these apartments were being leased very quickly and she further explained that once the apartment had been built I could view the property and sign an agreement.

The lady's name was Stacey. Stacey explained to me she would have to do a credit check which concerned me. I knew my credit history must have been pretty poor. However, I was here. If I didn't try I was never going to know. I really liked Stacey. We even shared some laughter. It just seemed every part of my life was falling into place. Everything in life happens for a reason. I am a strong believer that your destiny is mapped out, it's all in front of you. It's learning to understand what's placed in front of you, to make it of use to your life, if you so wish.

There seemed to be some chemistry between us. I looked at myself and thought I wouldn't stand a chance with someone so beautiful and an estate agent too. But maybe I was reading into things that clearly weren't there, and maybe it was something that I hoped would be there. Stacey was a truly attractive lady and dressed so elegantly she made me smile and gave me hope of a riverside apartment which I held out for and prayed that my wish would come true.

As the weeks passed I got into my training even harder. I was in the best shape of my life. I was 36 years old, fitter than I'd ever been, stronger than I'd ever been, mentally stronger than I had ever been in my entire life. I felt fresh. I could take on the world and win.

A very close friend of mine offered me some weekend work at a little bar called the Beckenham bar. This was a little wine bar in Beckenham. I didn't have a SIA badge. I wasn't legally allowed to work at the door but the owner explained to me that as long as I kept inside and popped to the front door occasionally he was sure things would be fine. I decided to take my friend's offer and I worked weekends, Friday and Saturday night, at the Beckenham bar which gave me a nice little wage. I became very close friends with one of the customers, Tony Evans. Tony Evans was a used car salesman who owned his own company in Croydon. I became really good friends with Tony. He was part of a TV series called Wheeler Dealers. Many years ago, Panorama had made a documentary regarding clocking cars and Tony was part of that. None of us have been angels in life. I really liked Tony. I explained to Tony I had been in the motor trade but not in a legal manner many years ago. We had a laugh and a good friendship was born. Tony said to me if I ever needed a decent car, to contact him and I could have the car on finance between myself and him. I said to him I would love that and if any nice cars came up I would be interested. Tony explained to me he had a lovely Mercedes coupe coming in that had my name all over it. I said, "Yet let me take a look as soon as it comes in, I would love to see it."

Life was beautiful. My mother was healthy, we were living life, paying bills and getting by comfortably. Why didn't this happen years ago? Why had everything come so late, but when I actually looked at the situation I believe sometimes in life you have to walk along that rocky road so to speak, to find your fulfilment in life and it just so felt this was my destiny. I was on the right road and hopefully with a nice shiny Mercedes to my name.

As the months passed the building plot of the riverside apartment was ready for viewing. Stacey telephoned me and explained I had passed the credit check. I was over the moon. I could have screamed with excitement. I actually stood a chance of living in a riverside apartment. What an opportunity I had been given and I passed the credit check with the strong possibility to rent in a beautiful Riverside apartment. I met Stacey one evening at the apartment for my viewing. I was so excited. Stacey took me through into the new apartment. It was brand new, everything was fresh, everything was bright, it was stunning. I absolutely fell in love with the apartment and Stacey looked amazing as if she had made a little bit more of an effort with her appearance that evening.

Stacey showed me around the whole apartment and explained to me if I wished to attend the office I could sign the lease papers for the apartment and then Stacey shocked me and said, maybe we could meet for lunch. For a split second which felt like eternity I was lost for words. How could this very beautiful lady wish to go for lunch with me? She was beautiful. She reminded me of a model from the 60s, just amazing. Of course, without a shadow of a doubt I said I would really like that and with that we set a date on which we decided an evening meal would be better. I was quite happy with female company even if it was just a meal or two as good friends. Just being on this new different journey was magical and to feel alive and feel attractive is something that is so important. I was in the best shape of my life, mentally and physically.

Since I changed my name it was as if the Gods opened new doors for me even if psychologically I just felt a new man. That was a great quality. Everything was falling into place, things just could not have been any better. Tony called me regarding the Mercedes and my viewing for the car was the following day. I started a great job earning good money, obtaining a beautiful riverside apartment to rent, and a lovely dinner date with a beautiful lady and the possibility of having a decent legal car, something I've never owned. Perfect, it's all just perfect.

Myself and Tony shook hands on the deal. I agreed to pay him weekly for the car. The money I earned from the door security work would pay for the car. Everything worked out perfectly. I had my lovely dinner date with Stacey, which was a lovely evening. I was quite happy just to sit with company of intelligence and beauty, it was all I was asking for. I was at the peak of my life. I felt I was a rich man in heart, something I had never felt before, something that I so wanted but could not obtain. I was on target to find a better place. Everything was just fine.

From time to time I would pop in and see my dear friend, Steve - the amazing friend that used to bring my mother up to me whilst I was serving my prison sentence. I saw a drastic change in Steve. He had stopped training and become a recluse and put on a lot of weight. This was happening over a period of time. I knew things weren't right between him and his girlfriend. He had left his wife for a girl. It was the worst thing Steve could have ever done as Chris, his wife, was a true lady with a true heart and truly loved and cared for Steve, but the disadvantage of working nightclub doors, was the offering of women which Steve took advantage of - he was a good-looking man and looked similar to Jean-Claude Van Damme, and was equally in good shape too but Steve had not trained in the gym for some time.

Steve was like a brother to me. My father loved Steve, my mother adored him too. He was a massive part of my life and my family. He had been with me on the journey during my drug years. However, Steve continued with those drug years. He didn't stop whereas I was forced to stop for the fear of it killing me.

One particular day a week before Christmas I decided to pop in and see Steve to take him some tobacco and a few items of food as he had become a recluse and never really left home. I never really understood mental health. Mental health was never spoken about with men. It was the same story as I mentioned before. 'Man up' get on with it was the attitude. I felt for Steve. I looked at a man that was broken but I couldn't see it. I genuinely could not see it. I couldn't understand why he had become a recluse. I failed to see the severity of his mental health. Steve told me he was using ample amounts of Diazepam and various other drugs to take him away from reality. I thought he had this under control. I thought this was probably just a bad patch and he would be back to normal in some time, but how wrong I was. I explained to Steve I would pop back to see him which would have been Boxing day. For some reason I never made Boxing day. Something came up so I decided to go and see him in the Christmas week. However sad news was brought to me when I met his ex-wife Chris by chance and she explained to me that Steve was found dead in his armchair, by his two daughters, on Boxing day.

With just those words alone, the sorrow, the sadness, the anger, everything boiled within me and the regrets came to the surface as I could see Steve was not in a good place but I didn't understand the severity of his depression, to the point of being suicidal.

Losing someone so special, so beautiful; my dear friend, Steve, was like my brother to me. He was ten years older than me. He was only 46 maybe 47 years old, still a young man with a whole life ahead of him yet the drugs had killed my friend. If this was not more of a wake-up call, this could have been me too, but I stepped out of that frame. I was lucky to realise that the drugs I was using were going to kill me at some point. Steve sadly never gave up the drugs and the loss and realisation of losing his wife, his true soulmate, killed him. If I had kept my promise that very Boxing day to pop in and see him maybe he would have still been alive or saved. It might have been me that would have found him dead. It was as if the Gods took my path away from that destination to go and see him that very day, but for his two daughters to find him dead was devastating beyond words. The loss of Steve in my life had a massive impact on me. I lost a very close friend due to drugs and depression. I lost the most beautiful friend of my life and I miss him terribly. How tragic! This was a massive drain on my heart and soul. I was in pieces. The day of the funeral was extremely hard as the opening music of the song will never leave me – 'Time to say goodbye' by Andrea Bocelli. This song I struggled to accept as it wasn't time to say goodbye, it wasn't Steve's time. Listening to that tune was a reality check once again how fragile life is and how it can beat you to your knees if you so let it. This could have been me, the thought of that running through my mind, the thought of my mother attending my funeral which was a very close situation at one point and one I could not put my loved ones through. I said to him in my mind, we will meet again my dear brother, this is not goodbye.

I struggled for a few months. I was still visiting my mother regularly and helping her from time to time with her little struggles. I got on with my work and just got to grips with life after losing someone so truly special. From time to time I met Stacey for dinner and we shared some laughter. Stacy explained to me that she was due to leave the UK for Australia with work prospects. Just having someone make me smile, the feeling of being wanted made me feel special. It was truly an amazing gift that Stacey gave me. We were just very good close friends and just having that in my life during the loss of Steve made me smile.

I realised despite someone being in a very dark place, if someone can make you smile just for a second, it's the most beautiful gift that costs nothing but means everything. Just to spend time with Stacey was lovely. There was nothing more in it. I was a gentleman, it was a part of me that was always there, where there were no jealousy issues, no issues if she was seeing someone else. Those questions whenever asked were the type of questions that Clive Sands would have asked, the paranoid drug addict. But not Rocky, he did not fear those issues because he was at peace with himself.

We kissed and had a cuddle and said our farewells. As I drove away I smiled with contentment that for that very short space of time that very beautiful lady made me smile; it was what my heart and soul needed to actually feel wanted, it was so beautiful, it made me feel special and that was all I wanted in life during my childhood years. I just wanted to be loved. I wanted someone to put their arms around me, hold me close and feel that spiritual energy between two souls of that magical feeling called love, with the energy that is far greater than anything in the universe. It was all I ever wanted, to be loved. I smiled as I drove away from Stacey and wished her the very best of luck with her job opportunity in Australia and that may God bless her with the smiles she so deserves after making me feel so special. I was so blessed.

The new chapter of Rocky Amore was here. As I turned the pages of my chapter and walked through the pathway of my journey my inner strength grew. I became a better person. I had not taken any drugs for a very long time and had no intention to go back down that same old road. I was on target to a better place, a better journey, to be a better person to live, to love, to laugh and appreciate every second you have with the people around you that you love.

My work with Ray looked in doubt. Ray had some difficulties with further contracts regarding his work with the council. I felt sorry for Ray as one particular day I saw him working with his son and I never saw Ray look so down. Ray was a man of his word. He didn't want to tell me he had no more work for me. I could see it in his eyes he was keeping me on because he knew I had a lovely flat, a lovely car and I was back on target but I knew the job had come to an end and it was time for me to move on. Due to my inner strength I knew that I could find employment if I so needed. My mind wasn't drug-induced. I wasn't suffering any paranoia issues. I had a clear mind and I knew if I needed it I could find employment again.

It was just by chance I bumped into to a dear friend called Neil. He asked me if I still was working for Ray and I explained to him I had finished work with Ray due to there being no work. He said he would have a chat with a friend of his called Anthony who worked in the motor trade. I said to him that it would be great if anything good came from that, it would be a blessing and I would really appreciate the mention.

Once again, I believe everything happens for a reason; the stages, the stepping stones are the progression of life. It is laid in front of you and my meeting Neil that very day was meant to be. I received a telephone call from Anthony mentioning he could supply me trade vehicles to sell. I had received a nice little sum from Inland Revenue from my tax return and with this I decided to go back into the motor trade legitimately to sell motor vehicles with a good regular supply from Anthony. This became my new job.

I met with Anthony and instantly liked him and I met his girlfriend, Tracy, and they were both truly genuine people. Myself and Anthony clicked straight away. He knew a little bit about my past I'm sure, but it didn't deter him and we became very close friends. As the months passed I wasn't earning the money I once was earning but I was still earning money. I had decided to do a little charity boxing match for a local children's hospice. I thought this would be a great way to do a little bit of something for the community and with that I started training for a boxing match which was held at York Hall in Bethnal Green. The training was going extremely well thanks to a very dear friend called James and that helped me prep for the boxing. Sadly, I had an injury and tore my quadricep off my knee doing a star jump. This was the most painful injury I've ever received in my life, to the point I was not able to walk for two months after a four-hour operation to reattach my quad to my kneecap. This was completely debilitating. Issues started to arise. I could not afford to keep my beautiful riverside apartment any longer and I moved back in with my mother once again. I believe everything happens for a reason in life. This didn't dishearten me. I was ok. I was strong enough to deal with situations that were laid in front of me.

As the months progressed my injury healed. After a year I began to have full movement in my knee and got back into my training again. I was selling cars like I was selling hot cakes thanks to Anthony's supply. The friendship with Anthony became very strong; in fact, to the point I would sit and have dinner with them and would go for a drink. I became close friends with his mother and father, and Tracy was an absolute diamond in looking after me and made me feel so welcome. I made two very good, true friends and they accepted my little faults from time to time. I was a bit impatient with things, with people from time to time. I didn't suffer fools very well but I was a better person. I was blessed that I had stepped back into a good place and I began working full-time with Anthony, picking used motor vehicles up from main dealers. It became a way of life and I absolutely loved working for them.

Whilst training at my local gym I got chatting to Sonia, a lovely lady that owned the gym with a guy called Adam. Whilst talking to Sonia she explained to me about a very dear friend of hers that she was at school with, that had been diagnosed with stage four cancer. This lady's name was Rebecca Watts and she had two young children, one of twelve and one of two years old. Sonia was almost in tears explaining to me the situation with her friend, Rebecca. I thought to myself how tragic this must be for a lady of just 39 years old to leave behind two children. As I proceeded to train that very day the thought of this tragic circumstance was playing on my mind and how it would have felt if I had lost my mother tragically. The thought of this played on my mind throughout the day, the evening and into the next day. I had never met Rebecca before, at that stage I never knew Rebecca. Sonia's story was extremely touching and I believed once again some things are meant to be and this very tragic story was meant to be told to me that very day.

I thought to myself why can't I put on a little event to help raise a little bit of money for the family to create memories for the two young children. I was on Facebook and I read their story through Rebecca's boyfriend, Richard. The story grabbed my heart. I could see some local families and friends trying to rally round to raise money for a magical holiday in Disneyland Paris. This just drove me harder to organise a little event and the idea came to me whilst driving past a haulage company, a vehicle recovery company called Neil Yates recovery in Snodland, Kent. I saw a beautiful American truck in their car park. This was a stunning American recovery truck, I thought! I spun around and drove back to look to see if I could talk to anybody.

I pressed the buzzer of the gate and at that a lady answered and I asked if I could come in and have a chat with someone regarding a little charity event I wished to put on. The lady let me in and I walked towards the beautiful American recovery truck. The wording Lonestar was above the window of this beautiful American truck. She was perfect. It said everything, it was meant to be. There was a guy cleaning his own truck. I proceeded to walk over to the guy and asked the guy about any chance he could ask if I could pull the American truck for a charity event for a very sick lady that had terminal cancer. This guy's name was Jason Amis. Jason was extremely helpful. We had a lovely, long conversation and he proceeded to explain to me he would chat to Neil Yates regarding seeing if it was viable for me to pull the American recovery truck for a charity event to help raise funds for a magical holiday for Rebecca and her two young children.

Mentally I was in a very strong place. Nothing in this world could break me. In fact I was inspired to see if I could create a wish to be granted for this family and bring a smile in such a devastating situation of a young lady battling stage four cancer and whether it was possible for me, physically possible for me, to pull that American truck over arm which I have seen on the TV of world's strongest men where you are seated on the floor with your feet pushing against a block and you pull with a rope with the hope to pull the truck or item in front of you for a distance. Could I do it? - was the question. I'd never tried this before. However, some years before, my friend, Andy Gower, had a strongman event where there was a 50-tonne truck to be pulled arm over arm by two strong men at the same time, and he asked me and another guy if we would like to test the truck out and pull it arm over arm. Myself and the other guy agreed that we would test it. Not for one minute did we think we would ever move it but we thought we would give it a go and behold! to our amazement we pulled this massive 50-tonne truck. So, with this in my heart and soul I knew I could move that 22-tonne American recovery truck. I would train my heart and my soul every day and prove to myself how strong I was mentally and physically.

I would not let this beat me, I would not let this surpass me, and this was my opportunity to give something back to life when I had taken so much from it. This was my chance to shine. I had spoken to Andy Gower of Evolution gym in Aylesford to see if I could put on an event on the same day he would do his annual truck pull event. I explained to Andy the situation with Rebecca and her two young children and asked if it was possible for me to place an event with him to pull this beautiful American truck. Andy said, "Absolutely no problem at all, absolutely no problem." So, I had a venue set. It was now just getting clearance from Neil Yates. Within a few days of organising the venue Jason telephoned me and said I had the all clear for the American truck to be pulled to place an event on for Rebecca.

This energised me. The spirit within me and the determination to help a young family with a wish, with a smile, to have a magical holiday and just be blessed with the time that was left for Rebecca to spend with her two young children and create a memory that was eternal, that would never leave her children and her loved ones and for Richard who also was fundraising for Rebecca - a lovely guy with a truly, lovely heart that stayed with Rebecca throughout her battling of cancer. His is one of life's true souls. With all this in mind it was time to make memories happen.

Unbeknown to me this was an opening of a door within my soul that energised something within me even more of what had been sleeping for a very long time. I trained my heart and my soul and gained a mass of following from people everywhere. This was the start of another journey for me. Everyone in life has a purpose which we all have a reason to be on this earth for - whether you become a doctor, a psychiatrist, a councillor, a surgeon, or a bin man, whatever makes you happy in life you have to follow your heart. We have one opportunity to live on this beautiful earth. It's down to us to utilise its beauty. Make life smile for others in their darkest times, turn tragedy into triumph and make a difference in other lives. This was the start of Rocky Troiani. Troiani was my mother's Italian maiden name.

Something was born once again. I still remained Rocky Amore but Rocky Troiani, The Trojan horse, was born with a view to help this family have a wish come true and the memory that would last for those two young children for the rest of their eternal lives. The venue was set, the truck was set and the date was set and a new journey ahead was also set for me. The Gods were showing me a new door that was going to be opened for me and this was the start of a journey that was my purpose, the reason why I was placed on this planet. Waking up in the morning and feeling alive is the most magical spiritual energy that's stronger than anything. It's like as if the universe is your strength and having faith and belief in yourself when you've come through a journey that's beat you to your knees yet you still stood back up and fought against all odds and you beat it. I felt alive. Rebecca gave me something truly special.

On various occasions I would meet Rebecca to give her progress reports on the fundraising. Rebecca had an energy that I'd never seen before. Rebecca smiled continuously which made me smile even though she was battling stage four cancer and chemotherapy, battling emotional stress with the knowledge that she was leaving her two young sons behind in this life. She still maintained a smile which made me smile, it made everybody else around her smile. Rebecca had an energy that was so strong, her eyes were big and beautiful. She made life smile despite the battling she was going through. She was a beautiful, spiritual energy that gave me the strength of a lion to fight for what you believed in and never give up despite the odds being stacked against you, to fight hard and smile at it at the same time. This was the opening of the door I was never going to look back on and for me to finally have a purpose in life. Not just to dig holes in roads to shovel concrete which is all fine if that's what makes you happy. But we have one life and one chance to live it; to wake up and do what you love the most. And for me to make others smile was my new journey.

Chapter 10

Discovering your Purpose in Life

Making someone else smile in life costs nothing. It's just taking a moment of your time for another person, a moment out of your day just to make someone feel special. I realised how amazing this feeling was for me. As a child, growing up, when I looked back over my years I discovered that love, affection and smiling was something I very rarely experienced.

Training for the truck pull was very meaningful. It wasn't just a strongman event for a trophy, this was an emotional journey contributing to create memories, laughter and smiles that were so desperately needed for this family. During this time, I was working with Anthony, selling cars. My work times were very flexible which allowed me to train daily for the big event.

I could never imagine for one minute how it must feel when you're told you have a limited time to live and knowing that you have children, young children that don't fully understand what the severity truly is, this must have been so daunting. Myself and Rebecca became very close friends, like a family and it was amazing. The funds were slowly ticking up. The goal was to contribute to a magical holiday for Disneyland Paris - something magical that the children and the family and loved ones would never forget.

This was a passionate journey, one that was going to lead me into a new chapter of my life. This wasn't just a charity event, this became personal. As the day of the big event approached I did become a little nervous as it looked like the event was going to be a very large public event as well as ITV Meridian news was present along with our local MP. It was going to be spectacular. Rebecca gifted me with an energy, a spiritual energy, something I didn't realise I had. It was amazing, seeing the excitement and the energy that was passing on to others from head shaving, sponsored walks and marathons, amazing how many people were getting involved. I loved the energy that helping others generates, inspiring other people to do good for others as we live in this rushing world of people not taking the time out for others when it costs nothing.

The day of the truck pull was upon me. The nerves I had the night before were terrible. I didn't want to fail this event in any way, not just from pulling the truck but from the fundraising - it just had to be perfect. I didn't want to fail this family. On my arrival at Evolution gym, the spectators were gathering. The barriers had been lined out, everything was in place, the truck was in place, which was the stunning Lonestar American recovery truck; she looked so beautiful there, and Jason Amis, the driver of the stunning Neil Yates recovery truck.

The atmosphere was electric, everyone sharing smiles and laughter. It was just amazing. Rebecca's friends, Grace and Annamarie, who I became very close to, and of course, Richard, Rebecca's partner, a truly lovely guy - everyone gathered for strength for this event for Rebecca. I had t-shirts made up with Rebecca's name on them along with the website page and link for the funding page.

Lots of my lovely friends came to support from all over the country. I was privileged and honoured that people took the time. Rebecca was the bright energy of the whole event, her amazing smile that blessed us to move mountains, specifically my knowing Rebecca's outcome would be heart-breaking so this event meant everything. All to contribute to a magical holiday just to make life a little bit easier with a smile and all it takes is a smile for someone to make their day feel special. This was my goal and unbeknown to me, it was to be the journey, the path for me to walk for the rest of my life. This made me feel alive, it lifted my soul and brought something to the surface, something I will never ever forget.

I grabbed the rope and placed myself, seated on the floor and looking down at 22 tonnes of American recovery truck with TV cameras upon me, the local press beside me and most of all, Rebecca, like an angel in my corner, right beside me with her two children. I took the tension out of the rope and with everything within me, with every muscle fibre, my sights set with Andy Gower right in my ear and along with the whole world which felt like it was looking up on me, I just did not want to fail. People had donated to see this happen, for me to pull 22 tonnes of American recovery truck, seated, with just my hands.

The roar from the crowd inspired my soul to move a mountain as I gripped and stood back. It felt like nothing was happening. I took all the tension out of the rope. As the rope was creaking under pressure I could feel everything within me cracking but then by the grace of God that scream from Rebecca, "Come on Rocky," the angels gave me the might I needed and 22 tonnes of American recovery truck started to roll forward. Once I felt momentum I pulled as far as I could back and came up as fast as I could forward to grasp the rope once again to pull. With all that and now the truck started rolling and she was not going to stop. My adrenaline was pumping through my veins at 100 mph. I had this and I achieved this and pulled 22 tonnes of truck, pulled twenty meters. My mother was there on the sideline shouting, "Come on son." Deep within my heart I wanted to make my mother proud of me, to show her I am a good person. I was not the nasty horrible little boy that I was told I was for so many years by a particular family member, ingrained in my heart and my soul. I believed I was this bad person and ended up living that journey for so many years. Showing my mother I was capable of doing something so special for a family that truly needed a smile in the desperate times of their life, was what I wanted.

On completion of pulling the 22 tonne American recovery truck, whilst gasping for air, I stood up with pride in my heart. Rebecca threw her arms around me in tears, thanking me. This was the proudest moment of my entire life. I felt blessed. I felt truly blessed knowing I'd made a difference in somebody else's life. It lifted something within me which I never thought I had, which brought to the surface who I truly was. It made me see within me I was a good person and seeing my mother proud in tears for her son for making somebody else's world a little bit happier. Seeing my mother looking at me so proudly made me feel superhuman and nothing on this earth or universe could take that moment away from me. It was a moment that was going to change my life, and one that I was never going to forget.

ITV Meridian news gave great coverage on the event along with the lovely Evolution gym that contributed so highly with capturing a crowd of people. Friends of friends and families, all attended, which made it a very special day a truly beautiful, unique day.

The two children, one of twelve and one of two years old, absorbed the atmosphere for their mother along with Grace and Annamarie, and all the beautiful and amazing friends that brought an energy only the Gods could deliver.

That very day showed my mother who I really was, what I was about as a human being on this planet and what my purpose intended to be. By witnessing the proud look upon my mother's face, something I've never seen before, this wasn't just a fundraising event; this was the birth of something very special, restoring a damaged childhood of child abuse physically and mentally for so many years by a certain family member. Within seconds the look on my mother's face showed her who I was. After the abuse I suffered for so many years suddenly I was pushed to the depths of my soul.

This day was a magical day and it wasn't going to stop there. I already had in mind another truck pull event. I wanted to make sure this family had their dream, their wish to go to Disneyland Paris, along with all the other fundraisers that spiralled along with the energy from this event that placed pennies in the funding pot, for this wish to come true.

Seeing Rebecca smile on that very day would never leave me. The energy that it gave me was amazing, beyond words and seeing my mother's smile as a result, was also such a spiritual feeling, a mixture of this that reinstalled and reprogrammed the computer within my mind. In life we have choices; tragically other people or family members, jealous people whichever you wish to look at or call it, will try to take you away from your choice, your journey in life, your path, your destination, your purpose which is truly tragic in so many ways.

We are only on this earth for a very short space of time and not to make use creatively of this very limited time we have on this earth is extremely sad. To wake up in the morning and do a job you really don't want to do, to wake up in the morning and not fulfil your heart with happiness from something that you love to do, is meaningless. It's an empty journey with no fulfilment.

I was becoming that lost soul on a journey that had no purpose. It was meaningless with no fulfilment. Yes, some work that I did, I enjoyed, but it didn't give me that fulfilment of purpose. I wanted to wake up in the morning and feel alive for the day, blessed by the grace of God, to be given an opportunity to realise a destination can be obtained through taking the right path, by having the right people around you, essential to your journey. I had surrounded myself throughout my life, specifically my teenage years into my twenties with the wrong people, people that drained my goodness, that used my kindness and showed me no loyalty or morals in their wrongdoings towards my nature.

This new chapter gave me true purpose. I loved making people smile. I was born again within me. I was recreated. Clive Sands was laid to rest some time ago and Rocky was born. That wish to make other lives better, for those that suffered in whichever form that may have come, from a terminal illness or simply just a smile for a day out and to tell someone how much you care or how beautiful they look - a simple smile.

The very day of that truck pull gave me so much and I was going to live and breathe, helping others, and Rebecca gave me this energy. And with this in mind I planned the second event for Rebecca and her children to go on a magical holiday which they so deserved, to create a memory for them all in this life and the next life.

The second event and date was set, for me to pull all 44 tonnes. Once again it was arm over arm, seated on the floor; a massive, heavy goods vehicle with a tank and armoured vehicle placed on the back of the truck. Now this was going to look impressive and bring another smile for this family. I had not fully recovered physically from the previous event but I wanted to carry on while the energy was still alive, whilst people were still intrigued to see whether I could move a mountain of 44 tonnes, almost double the weight of the first truck. I had to keep the energy alive directly after the first event. I didn't want things to go stale or people to forget the purpose of these events.

Rebecca was still in relatively good health or so we were led to believe by her smile which covered a multitude of feelings. Rebecca's smile is something that would always stay within my heart. It was so meaningful but behind the smile I knew of Rebecca's sadness, the devastation, the soul wrenching feeling that she knew possibly within the next few months she was no longer going to be with us. Knowing this, I could only imagine it being truly soul destroying. I cannot put into words what I was witnessing as I have never experienced seeing a family having to prepare for death specially when children are involved or even in some situations when children are of an age at which they understand.

How do you come to terms with your parting so soon, when everything is out of your hands, there's no control? This was my first taste of witnessing this, and one that I learnt so much from and that life is extremely fragile and none of us know what tomorrow brings. None of us can prepare for such a devastating journey and everything is out of your hands, specially when an illness is terminal, such as stage four cancer. Your life - if it's destined for one path and that's the next life.

I have always had a strong faith. My mother was Roman Catholic. I've always been surrounded by faith. I believed there was something else, another world, maybe another energy whatever that may be, but always believed there was something else. None of us know for sure, none of us can be certain but if you believe there is an afterlife and that makes you feel better with that understanding, then use that energy. None of us knew exactly the time left with Rebecca as there was a point we all knew it would be farewell and, for me, in the short space of time that I knew Rebecca, it was as if we had become a family. It wasn't just a charity event; we became a family, a unit of strength, of love. I loved Rebecca, I loved her children, I loved her friends - this wasn't just a simple charity event to raise money. I wanted to give them something beautiful, something which was missing in my life, and to give something to another life which is truly special in so many ways.

The second event was underway, everything was in place – barriers, and again, ITV Meridian news created awareness for the fundraising page as well as support from the general public. That was a great help regarding funds which was going to make this wish come true for Disneyland Paris. This was a cold December morning. Thankfully the rain held off. The ground was all swept of stones and debris as I didn't want the wheels to grab a stone from underneath which would stop me from pulling the truck since it was double the weight of the first truck and everything had to be spot on. The crowds were amazing - heaps of spectators, other gym owners came, Sean Kennedy from Reps and Sets gym, Gravesend, Andy Gower from Evolution gym, Paul Knight Crayford Weights and Fitness and, Tanya, his lovely wife - these two amazing people that supported me throughout my very dark days whilst in prison, and Stephen McNeil who originally taught me how to pull an articulated lorry with his strongman experience which was a true asset.

The whole event was masterfully planned like a perfect game of chess, everything was in place. It was just down to me to pull 44 tonnes arm over arm with an army tank on the back of the lorry as well as an armoured vehicle. It looked terrifying but I had one mission and that was to fulfil a wish.

My lovely, dear mother was on the sideline once again, supporting me and a particular family member that I really didn't want there was also present; the very same person that made my life hell from childhood. I could see there was no real reason to be there for this particular person other than to see me fail. This drove me more to succeed, to prove to that person I was not a failure in life, I am a success, I will succeed in whatever I set out to do. Make or break, I was not going to fail.

Once again, I took the tension out of the rope and then pulled back to the point where every joint of my body was creaking and cracking. The rope was cracking under pressure - 44 tonnes of steel along with 26 wheels to rotate - of friction along a concrete path. As I took the tension, nothing at all happened. No matter how hard I pulled nothing was happening. I held on for dear life that rope with all the grace of God and every angel behind me, my heart and soul was praying for movement. All I can remember was the words of Andy Gower telling me it will feel like nothing's happening but once you get past that inertia, the feeling of nothing is happening, once you get a slight rotation, then don't stop or let go. I was very blessed with some very experienced strong men as friends that guided me with their advice.

Eventually by the grace of God, with the screaming of Rebecca who decided to sit up into the cab to inspire me, as my eyes were transfixed on Rebecca in front of me, above me in the cab of the lorry, I could see her smiling. The energy that she gave me was electric. Once again it was like a spirit and entered my soul and lifted every muscle fibre within me. I could see Rebecca screaming and shouting, "Come on, you can do it." And those wheels moved.

The Impossible was made possible and 44 tonnes moved. The roar from the crowd and the energy was amazing, beyond anything I've ever experienced in my life. Rebecca jumped out of the cab along with her two children and once again wrapped her arms around me. Once again another moment that will never leave my soul knowing you have created smiles for people in such a desperate world that they were living in, just showing a little light at the end of a very long, dark tunnel - this was the moment I realised even more so who I was and what I was destined to be and not what I had become due to the person that done me so much damage and broken my spirit and stamped all over it. I was alive more than ever.

The owner of the tank suggested why not have a spin around the block in the tank with Rebecca. This was a momentous memory that I would so take with me into my old age. I asked if that was possible and with that the lorry driver manoeuvred the lorry so we could take the tank off and for the owner of the tank to take myself and Rebecca around the local streets and just scream at the top of our voices and enjoy the memorable moment.

As myself and Rebecca stood at the top of the tank in our little slot where we both stood with the driver in the front in his little slot, he proceeded off onto the main roads with myself and Rebecca standing proud at the top of the tank with our arms in the air smiling, cheering, laughing, as we drove onto the main road in this massive tank. I remembered looking over at Rebecca, arms waving in the air with joy. I took a moment to look into her eyes and for that moment she had forgotten about her cancer, for that moment in time and for those minutes that we were blessed with, I took the time to note the energy and the happiness of Rebecca. That valuable specific moment in time where Rebecca forgot about everything and she enjoyed the moment, that happiness, the joyful feeling of feeling alive, gifted with life.

I could not take my eyes off Rebecca; this was meant to be. This was my purpose and to know that Rebecca forgot about everything albeit for those minutes was something that Rebecca would not have experienced if I hadn't turned around in the gym that day and spoken to Sonia. That very moment of forgetting her cancer would never have happened if I had just carried on with my normal day, not taking the time to think about another person. That moment in time, it all would never have happened. So, for me to think of another which didn't cost me anything other than my time and energy - what a magical gift to give to someone in such a dark place in their life!

For those minutes, seconds and hours, Rebecca forgot everything and just enjoyed the crazy moment of us both screaming at the top of our voices standing at the top of this tank, truly victorious. We were winning and we would not give up on what we believed in. We were victorious and for those beautiful moments, for a memory captured for me that moment, was my gift to me, that moment in time in that tank with Rebecca as we went round those roads, people piping and tooting and waving - for me that was my gift to my spirit to feel alive in my soul, that was my reward and a memory that will stay with me until the moment I close my eyes on this world. That memory will stay with me until my last breath on this earth and it will never leave me, because I made Rebecca smile, and that was the most priceless gift that Rebecca could have ever given me. That magical smile was going to stay with me for the rest of my life on this earth. So, God bless your soul, Rebecca Watts, because you gave me life, a reason to wake up in the morning and live my life with an energy that helps other people smile in such dark times. You blessed me with a beautiful gift which will never leave me.

Sadly, we knew the day would be approaching us. While working at the car site I received a telephone call from Grace. The telephone call was one I was dreading but knew at some point it was going to come but I didn't realise it was going to be as soon as it did. Grace proceeded to tell me whilst crying, trying to grasp the energy to tell me the tragic news, that Rebecca had sadly passed away. I sat down in the workshop alone and Grace explained to me that she was there as Rebecca slipped away and that even at the very moment of leaving this life Rebecca still maintained a smile with her tears and the fight to stay for her young children. Rebecca was a remarkable lady. Words could not express, how remarkable Rebecca truly was!

Rebecca was an angel that walked amongst us. This angel was now on a journey to heaven, an angel that was taken from her family too soon due to cancer, a very cruel disease that takes people of any age, and Rebecca so young and had so much to offer. My thoughts drifted to the memory of myself and Rebecca whilst in that tank, driving around those streets, as I recalled that moment and realised that I would be looking back on that moment and thinking to myself -was this the last time I was going to see Rebecca smile with her beautiful energy? those beautiful big eyes that had an energy of a spiritual nature, that made you smile too. Truly missed, beyond all words.

Whilst crying on the phone to Grace I proceeded to tell her I would never leave their side, I would never leave the children's side. The two young boys that had lost their mother. Like promising my father, I would look after his wife, my dear mother, was a promise that I did break but I had the opportunity as my mother was still with me in life. I at least had a chance to repair the past. I was blessed with the opportunity to make a difference in the forthcoming years with my dear mother and by doing the charitable work that I had been doing. It made my mother proud.

As I came off the phone with Grace, I sat back in my car and cried and reflected on the moments of laughter that myself and Rebecca shared and her two young children. As I was reflecting over the memories a beautiful robin flew and sat on the door mirror of my car, a beautiful little red robin. This had never happened to me before. I had sat in the car many times at the car site to have my lunch and never had this happened. This beautiful, little red robin was Rebecca thanking me for her smiles. She came to me that very day, that very moment whilst I was crying in my car. That beautiful red robin came to say 'thank you'. I strongly believe that with all my heart and soul, that was Rebecca. How beautiful, how special and how truly uplifting, and restoring the belief in the afterlife, as they say robins are angels of loved ones and that very moment proved how very true that was. The little robin flew away but left me with a smile and lots of beautiful memories of some beautiful moments lived.

If I had walked away that day out of the gym, not taking notice of what was in front of me and even if I had not gone to the gym that day none of those memories would have been made or created. None of those smiles, none of that happiness or hope or belief, none of that day would have happened. If I had not taken the time to think of another no smiles would have been created. Lives were changed for them all and this gave me so much of a purpose, to know I changed other people's lives - it's the most magical that my soul could have received in all the years of my life. It was as if I was born again from the moment I changed my name and cleansed my soul which changed my destination. Rebecca, you will always live within my heart and my soul, and I love you with every beat of my heart. I live with your memory within me and until we meet again I will live to keep your legacy alive. And that magical smile that you gave to everyone else, I will keep that smile alive for you and your children, and once again that is a promise.

Chapter 11

You have my Heart in your Hands

L osing Rebecca opened my eyes to what can be expected when helping these families. I quickly realised when I took on a mission to fund raise for a family or an individual I was subjecting myself to heartache. I realised I put my heart and soul and my emotion and passion to succeed behind every case I was to take on. With the emotion and passion that I put into the cause I would love the family too, specifically, the individual that I was fundraising for. This made me very different from other charities or individuals fundraising for other people.

Fundraising for Rebecca was an experience that will never leave me. Attending her funeral was extremely painful, witnessing her loved ones, specifically her two young children only one of whom attended the funeral due to the two-year old being too young to understand. Alfie, the older son, was devastated beyond words. I said to myself, within my heart I will always be there for children.

For a period of weeks, possibly months, I was in a little bit of a dark place, but within that time, I had made a decision. I would further help others whether it is sick children, terminally ill children or the elderly, for a wish come true, for a day out down the coast, a meal or just a simple smile for their day for those that need it. Even as a child I was starved of something which was magical and that was love. Although my mother and father loved me in their own way, affection was not shown. It was just that generation and how it was during the 70s and 80s. So, with this in mind, knowing that some children that would lose their parents due to a terminal illness which was also starving them of the love of a parent.

This feeling played on my mind a lot and I knew how that felt. Even though I had parents the lack of love and affection played a part in my character as a person. Knowing of this feeling, the thought of another person or child being starved of a magical gift called love was something I was aware of. Even if it was just simply taking time to make that person smile, it just made their day a little bit brighter.

I had a mindset for the journey ahead. And this journey ahead was going to make a difference in people's lives. Using my experiences in life, the child abuse that I received from a family member, the emotional battering of my spirit which made my life hell - all these experiences and the discovery of myself during my prison sentence - I was going to put all into one pot and make good from a negative part of my life and turn it into a blessed existence which would make my mother proud. I made sure I kept in regular contact with Rebecca's family and friends, and wanted them to know that I am there if they need me.

One thing I did learn from this whole experience and a very valuable lesson at that, was that talking can be very cheap. People will say a mixture of words to make you feel better which to a degree is nice but to maintain those words in the heart. Actions speak louder. I was a man of my word. If I tell you I am going to be by your side, by your side I will stand. This was a quality that became stronger within me. The thought of someone else feeling sadness and loneliness during a very dark time in their life is a feeling I used to feel as a child, isolated and lonely.

Having true people in your life is essential to your journey to reach your destination. During this time, I became very good friends with a wonderful guy called Clinton Beadle. Clint for short. I met Clint at a local gym where we trained. Clint would call me from time to time for a chat as a friend and also helped me with event training now and then.

During life's journey you will meet an abundance of people, some just associates and some will become true friends. As I was getting older my circle was changing. In fact, my circle was getting smaller but with this in mind, I realised those that were left within my circle were my true friends. People recognised me for what I did for Rebecca and my Facebook social media page became busy with very kind messages which were truly inspiring; messages that will stay within my heart forever.

During this time of my life my social media interaction became very active and with this the odd kind remark from various ladies would appear. But one that caught my eye was from a lady called Daniella. I thought I would try my hand at dating but it is something I hadn't done for a very long time. I was so out of touch with dating, it had been such a long time but was worth a try to see how I feel. On the first meeting with Daniella she came across extremely sweet. For a period of time, now and then, I would meet Daniella for a little dinner and chat; it was lovely to have some female company.

There was a little space in time where I simply got on with work at the car site and took a little time to re-adjust after fundraising for Rebecca, a little healing time. I was then approached by a friend who knew of a family that needed support in fundraising for a very sick little baby. I wasn't quite ready emotionally but I wasn't one to walk away from a situation for a family that may have needed some help and support. I looked into their case and decided to help and with this I organised another truck pull event. I decided to meet the mother of the child in question with a view to help, support, with regard to fundraising. The baby was terminally ill. There was no cure. As such all I could do was financially support and help with fundraising for a special wheelchair for the child for days out and other amenities that would support and help the baby throughout the time the little one was with us.

I got my head down back into the gym again and trained hard to attempt to pull fifty tonnes of two recovery trucks supplied by Neil Yates. Neil Yates' recovery became a fantastic support for my charity work and Jason Amis always gave his time for any event training that I needed to do prior to the event. I organised a gofundme page with a view to raise funds for this family and proceeded to train and put my heart and soul once again into helping a family that desperately needed support.

Myself and Daniella became close and entered into a relationship. My mother quite liked Daniella - she was a bubbly spirit, full of life. I was far from an easy person to have a relationship with. My insecurities came back and were beyond repair, but I had to try and open up and start dating. It's been years since I let anybody close to me emotionally. I was exceptionally cuddly. I had to hold hands all the time to feel secure, for the need to be loved. This became an annoying attribute of mine which I realised. The need to continuously be told 'I love you', those magical words I so desperately needed within my heart that was so starved for so many years and the lack of understanding of those words was a desperate measure to feel loved.

I kept my head into my training with the view to fundraising for a very sick little baby. I was very good friends with one of life's true souls, his name was Joe Egan. Joe Egan was a former professional heavyweight boxer and trained in the Catskills as a sparring partner for Mike Tyson when Mike Tyson was in his prime.

Joe Egan was set to attend my event which was to be held at a gym called Bulks which was in Gravesend in Kent. I love Joe Egan, a larger than life Irishman, who was nicknamed by Mike Tyson as 'The toughest white man on the planet'. During sparring sessions with Mike Tyson, Joe Egan could not be put down on the canvas. Mike Tyson's sparring partners very rarely ever lasted two sparring sessions. Out of a series of guys that were taken to the Catskills, every single one of them took a beating and was laid on the canvas. Joe Egan was the only one that took every punch from Mike and with this they became very close friends. I was blessed with Joe's friendship and his attendance to help support my event and bring awareness with Joe's popularity. It was one that would bring a bigger audience to support a family and a baby that was battling for his life.

I also became very close friends with the family and would regularly take funds to the family which had been fund-raised and every single penny always went to the family that was given to me. That was a big issue with me - that every penny went to the family. The gofundme page was reaching good figures and everything was on target and a boxing event was also to be laid on thanks to our local hero of Medway Towns by the name of Johnny Armour, a former three times, welterweight champion of the world - another very dear, close friend of mine that was in great support of this event and attended in person with his world championship belt.

The support didn't stop there as another well-known heavyweight professional boxer was also there to attend, by the name of Matt Legg. Matt Legg was a fantastic professional heavyweight that stood toe to toe with some of the world's best in the ring and one of them was to the name of Anthony Joshua. I was set to have an exhibition bout with Matt Legg after my attempt to pull two articulated recovery trucks. I was hoping my arms were still in one piece enough to stand a few rounds with Matt Legg. Also, Shaun Smith, very well-known from TV documentaries, for his debt collecting skills, a truly great guy.

The whole event was looking spectacular with some amazing support from some amazing people. My mother was so excited with this event as the previous ones that I laid on for Rebecca. My mother wanted to be there for this event which made me feel proud and blessed that my mother could witness her son doing something positive things with his life and making changes to his journey and his destination. This was very passionate, very deep within me, I wanted my mum to feel proud of her son helping others in desperate times of their lives.

Myself and Daniella sadly were not getting on too well. I was not an easy person to live with. I struggled with being in a relationship and this was incredibly unfair for Daniella. One thing I didn't like doing in life was making someone feel rejected or unloved which were all those emotions I lived with daily within my heart and soul. I was not at peace within myself to be in a relationship but we thought we would keep going and see what the outcome would be. As life goes on, I am learning an awful lot about myself. As we get older we live with experiences which either make us stronger or break us. Life's experiences are wisdom gained. Wisdom is an art of life and it should be used with great care and respect.

Hurting people we claim to love, is a very dangerous game, and that was something I was definitely not into. I was feeling incredibly guilty with the way I was with Daniella and planned at some stage to express my feelings and was hoping it would come across the right way but it very rarely did with me. It would come out in an aggressive manner, normally an argument. I was hoping I could deal with this situation calmly and amicably.

The day of the event was upon me. Everything was set, the ring was set up, the trucks were set up and the crowds were pouring in - what a magical day! My beautiful friend, Grace, bought a small chair for my mother to sit on so she could watch her son perform his magic and strength while sitting comfortably with a view for my wish that my mother be proud of her son.

Everything I have ever attempted in my life I have failed at. I tried little businesses, nothing ever worked. My relationships always failed. Everything I attempted to do was a failure. For the first time in my life I found a journey and a passion for something I was good at. Maybe this was my destiny, my final destination, to do something I loved and was passionate about - helping others in desperate times of their lives. Life is not a journey as they say; it's a destination and I felt I'd finally arrived at my destination. An amazing guy was my MC for the day. His name was Martin C. My mother danced with Martin at my last event for Rebecca. Martin is a bright spark of life, he has an energy that brings smiles and he made my mother smile that day by making her feel special by dancing with her. That was a memory logged in my mind. That was a beautiful gift to me. Knowing a smile was made for my mother that day was a beautiful memory for me.

As these events progressed I was gaining beautiful memories for me; smiles that had been made for families that desperately needed them. Knowing you have taken a moment of your time to change another person's life with a view to making it a little bit better even if it's just a smile was magical for me and rewarding in so many ways.

I was learning very quickly the positivity that this was creating with people around me, inspiring others to do good, to take time for others. A smile is infectious even when you struggle to smile yourself. Knowing what's behind that smile can be very painful at times, but for that person to create a smile for you and for you to create a smile for them costs nothing.

The event on the day was magical, everyone laughing, everybody smiling. I struggled to move the two articulated recovery trucks. They wouldn't move no matter what I did, how hard I pulled, the struggle was beyond measure. The moment I pulled the first truck, by the time the tension was taken up on the rope on the truck behind, it was like trying to pull Mount Everest. It was barely an inch moved and this took me all of 30-minutes tension pulling with my arms, pushing with my legs, arm over arm. I was drained of every inch of energy. Something was missing within me that day. I didn't realise the damage I was doing to myself over Daniella. I wasn't the normal Rocky Troiani that day. It was as if my spark was taken from inside me. The heart was not in it and that affected my training as well as the event to pull the two articulated lorries on the day. The week before I had pulled fifty tonnes of one articulated unit successfully but by the time I took on this event I was drained emotionally. I beat myself up, inside.

My second event for the day was to step in the ring with the one and only, former professional heavyweight boxer, Matt Legg. My friend, Mickey, was taping my hands up. He said to me, "Are you sure about this?" as Mickey was a former professional boxer himself and had watched Matt Legg on the pads and Matt looked fierce. I have to say I was not looking forward to the prospect of getting punched around the face as my arms were hanging off their sockets after trying to pull fifty tonnes. I prayed that Matt would take it easy with me.

As I stepped towards the ring, my mother and Daniella were at the side of the ring shouting my name and there was a moment there that my mother was shouting, "Come on, Troiani." Just that moment alone made me feel amazing. My mum was cheering my name. If I got knocked out in the first round I didn't particularly care as my mother was proud of me and she was a great boxing fan. It was just great just to see my mother enjoy herself and smile.

As the first bell went for the first round, I just kept my arms up and threw a few punches but realised within seconds, Matt was taking it easy with me and thank the Lord above he did. It was great fun, it was just a very gentle sparring session and one that was a momentous moment in my memory for when I get old - I could say I stepped in the ring with Matt Legg albeit a very gentle exhibition. Matt was a gentleman in the ring as a gentleman in life. The event was a true success and one that will never be forgotten and raised thousands for the family.

I had fallen ill with an ear infection and some kind of virus which laid me up in bed for a couple of days. Whilst in bed I thought I would take a moment to call my mother and see if she was ok. I must have called at least several times with no answer, which concerned me. This was playing on my mind severely and I could not rest until I checked if my mother was ok. I managed to get out of bed and put on my clothes and drive down to my mother's just to double check she was ok as I had a horrible gut feeling something was not right. My mother never not answered the phone. Even if she had missed a call she would call me back, so this was unusual and I had to find out to have peace of mind.

As I pulled up to park I could see my mother's curtains were still drawn at 10:30 a.m. in the morning. My stomach sank, my anxiety and adrenaline, was of pure concern. This was completely unusual for my mother's curtains to be drawn at 10:30 a.m. in the morning. I approached the front door and it was still locked. Luckily, I had a key and I opened the door. The lights were still on from the night before and there were no signs of life. If I completely feared the worst, this was something that I had been feeling for some time, just the thought of losing my mother would destroy me and I would never be the same person ever again. My mother was my life, she is my life, she is my entirety.

As I walked into the room I could see my mum's feet on the floor. She was lying flat on her back. I screamed to my mother and shouted, "Mum, are you ok? What's wrong?" She didn't move. I was in a pure panic state and then I saw my mother's eyes moving. I managed to pull my mother up off the floor. She was in a terrible state. It appeared my mother had fallen over whilst closing the curtains. She could not get back up off the floor and she had lain there all night long.

This broke my heart. I could not see my mother like this ever again with the fear of her falling over and hurting herself. Her legs were getting weaker as she was getting older and her balance was a little unsteady. With this in mind I moved in with my mother to look after her and care for her and maintain the promise I had made to my father. It would break his heart if he could see this. My objective was to look after my dear mother from now on and make sure whatever it takes I would make sure she is safe and well and never comes to any harm.

My relationship with Daniella was under a serious strain and sadly we parted. I knew we would end up arguing which was totally down to me. I was not ready for a relationship and it was unfair on Daniella to put her through any further emotional stress. I was focussing deeply on my charitable work which had taken up an awful lot of my time. I was hours upon hours on social media as well as training for these events. I was leaving Daniella out and not paying her the attention I should have done. Finding my mother on the floor after she fell over and myself spitting up with Daniella, it was as if things were meant to be that way for that moment in time. I moved back in with my mother to become her carer.

Once again, I believed in life some things are meant to be. We are shown a path. To fight against that path sometimes could lead you down a very different avenue where you shouldn't be. You have to look out for the signs that are put before you in life and take note and be vigilant. The shock of finding my mother on the floor and moving back in with her was a new page once again. I lost contact with Daniella. We shared the occasional message. Deep within my heart, I sincerely wished her the very best in life and simply wanted to apologise for being me. My mother was happy to have me home with her. She was sad that Daniella and I had finished our relationship. I knew by me being at home beside her she felt safe once again and that gave me comfort that the promise I had made to my dear father - for whatever years my mother had left on this earth, I would be by her side every minute of every second of every hour of every day – was fulfilled. I was not going to leave my mother's side from this point on.

Further tragic news came to me by telephone call from the mother of the little baby that we had been fundraising for. I was asked by the mother if I wished to say farewell to the little boy. I felt it my duty as I had put all my heart into the event I did for the little lad and wanted to say farewell personally. I purchased a small St Christopher for him to hold onto in his tiny hands to take into the next life. The mother had met me at the children's hospice called Demelza Children's Hospice. The mother walked me into a very tiny room where the little baby boy was laid to rest. This little room was called the ice room. It was freezing cold, like a fridge. As I opened the door I could see a single bed. The wall paper was so colourful and bright, a pretty little bedroom with cuddly toys all around the room.

The room had a certain scent, one that would never leave me. As I walked into the room I could see a very tiny baby lying in the centre of the bed. He was so small, so tiny, the room was freezing cold and my heart was devastated as I had never witnessed a child that had passed away. I have never witnessed anything like this in my life. My heart was devastated for the mother the way I was feeling at that moment in time. I was in pure shock. My dear friend, Grace, came into the room with me and we shed many tears.

People never knew of this side of the charitable work that I was doing for the sick and terminally ill children. All they ever see was the event on the day, full of smiles and happiness but what they don't see are moments like this of witnessing a child that has passed away at only two years. This vision will never leave me.

It's moments like that when you question faith in God himself. "I ask you, why are you taking these innocent, little lives? What have they done so wrong on this earth to suffer so badly?" I questioned faith when Rebecca had passed away. I questioned faith that very day. That little baby lying in that very large single bed holding onto a little St Christopher that I placed into his hands and questioned, "Why dear God? Dear Lord, why are you taking these lives? They have done no wrong to hurt nobody and yet they suffer in such a painful way; why take their lives?"

Once again, another funeral to attend, another soul lost I had been fund raising for, and I realised this was part of my journey of supporting these families that are suffering with terminal illnesses for children with limited life. I realised this was part and parcel of my journey. But one thing I did realise amidst all the heartache and devastation and tears; I realised that during the times of despair I created hope, I created smiles and laughter, of which memories were made that were going to last eternally and memories that would stay with us all for our lives ahead and for the families that were left behind. Memories were created that will live on eternally. This within my heart and soul gave me hope to carry on despite the heartache it created for me. And the tears that I will shed over these children and families, and for the beautiful people that lose their life to terminal illnesses.

To know I showed them love, genuine love from deep within my heart and knowing I lacked that magical emotion called love during my lifetime, I did not want anyone ever to feel the way that I felt during my hours of despair. I wanted other people to know I loved them. I was not going to leave their sides until they knew that smiles, hope and love were shown, and to care and hold their hands in times of despair.

Chapter 12

Let me bring you Every Kind Smiles

My charitable work was progressing fast. I decided to step back from the motor trade and take on a full-time path in helping others in desperate times. I looked into this prospect of registering a community interest company. I wanted everything legitimate, everything above board and to fundraise for projects and take this charitable work seriously as a business. Rebecca was a massive influence in my inspiration for charitable work. I sat and thought deeply as regards to what I would call the business. Everybody referred to Rebecca as Becks. The most memorable thing I had of Rebecca in my mind was her smile, her smile was extremely energising, spiritually it lifted you when you see her smile, her smile was electric beyond all words. Despite her situation in battling stage four cancer Rebecca smiled and that lives inside my heart permanently and without a second thought an idea of a name for the business sprung to mind.

Becks, I decided to change to BEKS, a similar short version of Rebecca but spelt BEKS, with the wording of Bring Every Kind Smile. It was as if this was meant to be a legacy of Rebecca to live on eternally and the smiles that she would radiate and inspire and bring the gift of an energy of a smile that Rebecca gave. This will live on.

I registered the business as Bring Every Kind Smile, as a community interest company for non-profit. I wanted to make no money out of this charitable organisation. I wasn't naming myself as a registered charity but a charitable organisation strictly non-profit. I was to make nothing from the work that I was doing for others.

I asked for permission from the family members of Rebecca, young Alfie, and Louise, Rebecca's sister. They were extremely honoured that I would keep Rebecca's name alive with a view to helping other people in desperate situations in life from sick and terminally ill children right the way through to the elderly for a day out down the coast, a free meal, and simply a smile for their day.

I changed all of my social media and focussed it solely on the charitable organisation and set out for new projects to help others within the Medway community. I would consider anything that would help a family. Even just those that simply needed a smile. I knew I was opening up my heart to situations of further devastation in dealing with a lot of these cases. Some children were not going to see their next birthday and as well for the elderly and cancer patients this could be a journey that could deliver me a lot of heartache, but I was prepared to place my heart on the line for others if just one moment of their day I created a happy moment where it took them away from their devastation and their own heartache; if just a minute in their day a smile was made, then my job was done successfully.

My main priority was looking after my mother after finding her on the floor when she had fallen over. She had been there all night long. My mother's well-being was paramount and I made sure she was looked after, cared for and most of all, loved. I made sure daily I would telephone her during the day to make sure she was ok and that she had eaten.

I discovered from time to time that my mother would take her tablets in the wrong order. She was given blister packs for her medication and instead of taking morning, afternoon and dinner -which was down the pack correctly, she would take Monday, Tuesday, Wednesday and so on across the top of the pack and would mix her medication up. So, with this in mind I bought a daily pack where I would administer her tablets in the correct order so she could take her tablets correctly and safely. It was extremely important to me that my mother took her medication correctly. Life in general was blessed. I was blessed with the fact that I had my beautiful mother around me, and my wonderful daughter. What more could I ask for?

It became very apparent to me my childhood had affected my life. There were a lot of underlying issues that I hadn't dealt with and as time was going on through my later adult years I was discovering a lot more about myself. However, I was happy with what I was doing with my life regarding my career, running a charitable organisation that gave genuine love to the people that truly needed it - giving something that I was starved of, something I truly didn't understand but knew its beauty within. You don't have to know somebody personally to show them love. Love can come in many different forms. The energy that I wanted to portray was a love that cared and showed it cared and kept its word and never broke its promise.

I proceeded with new projects and came across a desperate family that was renting a small flat. I came across these people whilst watching ITV Meridian news. This particular family had a very sick little baby that was still in hospital but could not come home due to the severe damp conditions within the flat. They were in tears on the TV and wanted their baby to come home but due to the severe damp conditions the risk of infection to the baby was high. The baby was already battling a severe illness. The family could not unite as one to be a family.

With this in mind I found the parents on Facebook and contacted them directly to see if I could do something for them. I met personally the father, Stephen, a truly, lovely guy that desperately wanted his wife and his new born baby that had been battling an illness in hospital and was now fit enough, to come home. But his little baby was not able to do so due to the very severe damp conditions throughout the whole entire flat. I witnessed the severe damp conditions throughout and it was horrendous the landlord chose to do nothing to help this family, which was heart-breaking, as there should be strict stringent rules in place. However, sadly, even after continuous plying with the landlord to deal with the damp, nothing was done.

I set out to place a social media post looking for a team of people to blitz the entire flat and redecorate it and treat the damp conditions with a solvent that would keep the damp at bay. The response on social media was amazing. I got a team of people together and we blitzed the whole flat from top to bottom totally, redecorating the entire flat for them and treated the damp with chemicals that would hold the damp back.

If I say I am going to do something, if I set my heart on something to be achieved then I will not stop until that goal is reached. I wanted to obtain a reputation that was strong and as one that kept his word and saw a project through to the end successfully, and this was an extremely successful project and the whole flat was redecorated for free. I was very blessed for a local neighbour that worked in the management of a building company that donated all the paint required for this project.

The project was completed successfully and we said our farewells to Steven. It was an emotional farewell as he cried with joy and appreciation for what we had done as a team to redecorate his whole flat for him at no charge at all. For me, my reward is seeing the project completed and hope and faith and belief restored in a situation that was pure darkness. The BEKS Brings Every Kind Smile, our Rebecca, smiled upon this family. That very day her legacy spread smiles.

My reputation as a charitable organisation was growing. I was self-funded. I was still selling cars to pay for projects as I did not have a funding pot. I was financing BEKS with my own funds. Even with the previous project I purchased the rollers to paint the ceilings and walls as well as the brushes and dust sheets which all comes to money which I financed, myself. I was waking up in the morning with a purpose, with a reason and a passion which made me smile each day.

I then started having families contact me for help regarding helping other families that needed support and one of these was a family that lived in Faversham in Kent. My dear friend, Lisa, contacted me with a view to helping with just simply giving smiles for a family that had a little girl that was suffering an inoperable brain tumour. In situations like these the main objective is to create memories for the family, happy times to look back on and remember moments of laughter and smiles. There wouldn't be anything on earth that I could do that could change the outcome of the little girl but to create some happiness was my goal. I set out to meet the family and see what I could do.

I was looking to obtain sponsorship from companies or businesses that simply wished to help finance projects that are up and coming. Sadly, I obtained a lot of false promises none of which materialised to anything, people jumping on my back to benefit their own needs and which swiftly shut the door on any company or business but were not suitable as my reputation was at stake. I made sure they were gone.

Running a charitable organisation is a 24-hour a day job because you don't switch off. Even when you're sitting there on an evening, you're on a laptop dealing with social media responses and families and messages and calls. You never completely switch off but it was something I enjoyed doing. It was my love, it was my passion. It is my love and my passion and always will be too. I was still looking after my mother making sure everything was happy and well there and she would pop into the high street on a Tuesday and a Saturday to do a little bit of shopping which she thoroughly enjoyed. My mother was albeit a little shaky on her legs. She was still showing a lot of Independence.

I received many messages from many people, from many families that needed help. I could not deal with them all as there was only me. I had to make sure I was kind in saying that. Sometimes I just could not deal with everybody. But the ones I did choose to help, like a local family in Gillingham, sadly, almost lost their little boy to a brain tumour due to neglect from the doctors that kept passing it off as simple headaches. The little boy collapsed at the bottom of the stairs at home and his father, Lee, managed to revive him until the ambulance came to take him to hospital for further examination which revealed a brain tumour. Sadly, whilst the mother and the father in hospital were caring for their little boy further devastation was at their door. The mother, Kirsty, of little Georgie stayed with him in hospital and Lee returned home. As he opened his front door, in pure horror, he saw the whole entire ground level was flooded with water. It appeared an upstairs radiator had burst during their time in hospital with their little boy. Ceilings had fallen down, walls had collapsed, carpets ruined - every conceivable room from above and below was ruined.

After being contacted by a friend of Kirsty and Lee I decided to contact them with a view to see if I could help them. When I witnessed the pure devastation with my own eyes - no ceilings, no walls, no

Rocky Troiani

carpets, no floor - it was a shell of a house. A local builder promised to help the family. Sadly, the work was not getting completed and I could see the devastation in the father's eyes. He was a broken man. I had not met the mother of the little boy at this moment in time but my witnessing of the house in complete ruin and knowing of their little boy in hospital battling a brain tumour operation, I could not walk away from this project without trying to see if it was possible for me to obtain help in getting their house back together again.

I once again placed a social media post on my charity page on Facebook and with this I received an abundance of offers but one in particular stood out a mile. His name was Richard Sandman of R Sandman builders. I met Richard at the house to view the project as this was something far beyond my means. I am not a builder. I can barely paint with a brush. This was a full refurbishment.

Richard was an absolute godsend and my first meeting with Richard was one of a friendship that would last eternally. The main quality I liked about Richard was that he kept his word on everything he said and set out to do what he did and completed it and he was very much like myself; he would not give up until the job was done. Richard had a wealth of contacts from carpet fitters to plasterers to electricians, everything at hand. He was a lifesaver and for me he was the one that managed to complete this project along with another amazing guy, Lee Carroll, who was a friend of the little boy's father. As a team we all pulled together and worked throughout non-stop. I funded various materials from plasterboard to coving to antibacterial paint.

During this time, we were battling a Covid pandemic and I had to obtain certain materials as the country was about to enter a complete lockdown. I purchased the antibacterial paint for little George's bedroom and thankfully the paint company gave me a discount due to the situation. During Covid lockdown, myself, Richard and the team continued to work throughout the day and almost into most evenings to complete this project for Kirsty and Lee and for little Georgie to return home.

The project was sailing on very successfully, and myself and the team decided to complete the loft conversion as a surprise for the family. Richard completely built the wardrobes for the bedroom, a seated area in front of the window, and made such a beautiful job along with Lee Carroll dealing with all the electrics. As a team we were formidable, unbreakable and passionate to make this happen for this family that tragically almost lost their son and also in the process almost lost their home.

Once again, the project was completed successfully and Lee and Kirsty brought their little boy home, and we all shed tears to a momentous moment. The BEKS charitable organisation had completed a successful project, once again winners, pure champions. Smiles were made, hope restored once again, and love created between people that had never met before. This is what I mean about sharing love. It comes in many different forms and the unity of love that was created on that day was magical, to see the smiles albeit tears of joy, the smiles were my reward as well as for all of us to see a family home safely with their little boy, by which he had time to recover from his operation and live to the best of their ability, happy.

I decided to help raise funds for the family. I would attempt to pull a double-decker bus 200m. This was going to be gruelling as there were no gyms open for training with all that. I had a local field to run around and steps to run up and down to keep fit. I had no strength training at all but had the heart and willpower to succeed and at least have a go at pulling a double decker bus 200 m which was pulling five times of 40 mm stretches one after the other. The event was a great success albeit very tiring and exhausting. Funds were raised for little Georgie and the family to help make life a little bit easier. It became notorious for me to do a truck pull or a bus pull or pull something incredibly crazy to help raise money for these families. I enjoyed the journey of the training involved as well as the success of raising funds for them all.

My plan was also to help the lovely family in Faversham in Kent with their little girl that sadly also had a brain tumour. However, tragically, this was an inoperable tumour, there was nothing that could be done for this little girl. I made a plan to meet the family and the little girl in question to see what I could do for them for a birthday surprise to bring a smile for the little girl and her family.

The little girl's name was Lyrah, just seven years old and the mother, Victoria, and her mother, Lorna - a lovely little family that just simply needed help and support in such a desperate heart-breaking time, and making the most of the time with their beautiful daughter, Lyrah. I wanted to create memories for them. I organised a long stretch limo to pick Lyrah and her mother up from the house with £700 spending money and a surprise trip to Hamleys Toy store in London. This was magical, just Lyrah seeing the Limousine pull up with bows and ribbons and spending money to her heart's content at one of the most famous toy stores in London. Hamleys Toy store was extremely lovely after my chat with them. They laid on everything for Lyrah at Hamleys and made her feel like a true princess. I knew this particular journey was going to be one that was going to pull on my heartstrings so deeply. I had lost a lot of years with my own daughter and I wanted to feel and see love in that little girl's eyes and make her feel like a true princess. I called her princess Lyrah. She was my little princess and I wanted to make her smile and create memories for her family that will never be forgotten.

I decided to do another truck pull to help raise funds for this family to make their time a little easier. I contacted Neil Yates recovery with a view to attempt to pull by harness 64 tons of articulated low loader truck. Once again, I contacted Jason Amis and also once again Neil Yates were exceptionally helpful and kind in supporting every truck pull I ever wished to lay on for families.

To train to pull 64 tonnes of a 26-wheel trailer is something I've never done before and once again we were doing this during a Covid lockdown, which had to be not a public event, just live feed on social media. It was impossible to get anywhere into a gym to train. I did the same as before, just run up and down steps to keep fit. I've lost a lot of muscle due to no gym training but what I lacked in muscle I made up for it in heart. I was not going to fail this truck pull and we raised in excess of almost three and a half thousand pounds of which £1,000 was donated by Neil Yates himself. The truck pull was a great success. Yes, I struggled to pull 64 tons but I did it. I placed Lyrah's little drawing that she had done for me - a beautiful coloured drawing of myself and Lyrah walking into the sunset – at my goal point. I treasured this drawing with all my heart, it meant so much to me. Lyrah always used to do me various little drawings and pictures to say that she loved me and thanked me for the things I did for her.

I treasured all of those pictures and drawings that Lyrah had done for me. I placed Lyrah's drawing at the end of the 25 m distance to pull the truck. I placed Lyrah's drawing where it was my point of vision, my goal, my focus point and I was not going to give up until I reached that drawing. As I pulled the 64 ton up the 24 m distance I screamed Lyrah's name out loud along the drive. The passion, the blood, the sweat, the tears, the anger, the love - every emotion of every step that I took of that 64 ton was coming out as a rage of love for this family.

Successfully I pulled 64 tonne full distance. I picked up Lyrah's drawing. I held it close to my heart. I kissed the drawing and said, "I love you, Lyrah, and this is for you." The love for this family for me was growing stronger and stronger. I thought the world of Lyrah. This was more than just fundraising for a family. They became my family once again. I opened my heart up to tears, but, in the meantime, I created smiles. I wasn't worried about my heart ache, it didn't worry me but for that moment in time, for that beautiful family memories were made, happy moments at Hamleys and a Limo full of toys, laughter, and just smiles upon smiles for them. For that moment in time they forgot their knowing the outcome of their little girl, and a little love and hope and belief was given.

Chapter 13
Pride of Britain

With every project I took on I gave these projects my heart. I would not walk away from anything until I succeeded, until the job was done. Other projects were ahead of me, in one of which I was dealing with an elderly gentleman that lived in Sheerness by the name of Arthur. A gang of burglars had broken into his home and beaten Arthur, pulled him to the floor and punched him. For a few pounds. An elderly pensioner of 75 years old. I was disgusted by what these creatures did to him. I saw his plea on ITV Meridian news. I could not walk away from helping that elderly gentleman that had given so much to society and that's how society treats him by throwing him on the floor and beating him up for a little bit of his pension money.

Once again, I raised just over £700 for him, just a little something to restore a little faith in his heart. On meeting Arthur, it broke my heart. His little flat had not been decorated for over fifteen, maybe twenty years. Arthur was a heavy smoker and all the walls were wet yellow. Arthur suffered COPD which is a lung disease and was permanently on oxygen to breathe. He could hardly walk any distance without getting out of breath. I decided to get a gang of decorators to decorate his whole flat for free to make it lovely and bright, so for whatever days that Arthur had left he could live in comfort with a beautiful bright, flat, all freshly painted.

The flat looked beautiful and the team successfully brought a smile for an elderly gentleman that was beaten and robbed, and again a smile restored hope and faith, and belief that there are good people in this world and for me to walk away knowing I gave that to Arthur was a beautiful smile made for me. Once again, I became very close to all the projects I took on, to the families, to the people, to the children and I decided to keep in regular contact with Arthur and make sure he was ok, from time to time, and show him love. I genuinely loved the old boy. As time went on I would be regularly contacted by people to see if I could help others for a smile and my dear friend of Nell's Cafe contacted me with a view to help a lovely, dear old lady that had one wish to come true and that was to feel that she was cycling along the seafront of Folkestone. The dear, elderly lady was residing in a care home in Folkestone. Her name was Molly. She was 95 years old and immediately I set out to make this wish come true to have Molly cycle along the seafront and feel alive and beautiful, and just have a wish come true. I contacted a Trishaw cycle company in Bexhill-on-Sea and a date was set along with a beautiful stunning classic Daimler limousine to take Molly in style to the meeting point of Bexhill-On-Sea where Molly would be taken, which was to be a surprise, in a three-wheeled cycle where Molly would be seated in the front of the cycle and the cyclist at the rear to cycle Mollie along the seafront.

On meeting dear Molly, I immediately fell in love with her. Molly was one of the code breakers in the second world war. She had an amazing history and with this I was going to make her wish come true to feel like she was cycling along the beautiful Bexhill-On-Sea seafront, to feel so special and once again to feel loved and cared for, and thought of.

We had cups of tea on the seafront in a lovely little cafe. We cycled along the seafront and the smile on Molly's face was absolutely magical. It was as if Molly was living her wish. It was beautiful to see Molly smile. It was just the most touching moment for me knowing that I created this BEKS, Bring Every Kind Smile. You are making so many smiles for so many people and wishes to come true. Lives that have been dealt tragic circumstances, just seeing smiles is a beautiful infectious experience that spreads amongst everyone present during that smile. A magical moment was made and Molly's own words were, "I will never forget this day." It made my day as, driving home, I shed a few tears of pure joy for Molly, knowing I had made her wish come true. I was the blessed one that day.

Life was becoming extremely busy with big projects such as another little girl by the name of Nellie Rose that was battling neuroblastoma. The family was required to raise £250000 for overseas treatment for little Nellie. I placed and programmed events for this family. They were such a lovely family and I loved them. My passion to succeed in every project was strong and I can safely say every project was a success and I wanted to contribute to help raise funds for little Nellie's overseas treatment.

I placed two events in the process, one was for me to pull a train. A Vangard locomotive and two railway carriages totalling 104 tonnes. This event was to be held at the East Kent Railway, a lovely vintage railway. This was for me to pull all this mass amount of weight along a floor ladder. Thankfully, the gyms had reopened and I was back training hard with a view to successfully pulling this train to help raise funds for this little girl. BBC News southeast had done amazing coverage on this for the day which was an amazing success. The weight of the train did not feel too much of a problem. I trained extremely hard for this event and the turnout of the public that supported Nellie Rose was amazing, beyond words. My dear friend and former professional boxer and close friend to the great Mike Tyson, the one and only, big Joe Egan came to support the day, and as always Joe so brought an amazing crowd of people of support and strength that was given for this event.

Support was growing strong for BEKS and people from far and wide began to know of this little community interest company. However, at this time I still had no sponsorship and was funding all the projects from my own pocket. Thankfully I had gained a true mass of support once local businesses realised what my objectives were, along with my reputation which was extremely good. Many businesses would help with equipment for events. Another major event also was taking place for me to train for a 30-hour long stop to beat the record of Joe Wicks who trained non-stop for 24-hours for Children in Need. My goal was to smash this and train solid for 30 hours non-stop thanks to the amazing support of my very dear friends, Paul Knight and Tanya, who own Crayford weights and fitness. The support was amazing and once again my lovely friend, big Joe Egan, was there to support.

The support and energy for that event was amazing and a fantastic amount of money was raised for little Nellie Rose and her family. I absolutely love this family and the little girl has such a character about her that she made everybody smile. These children despite battling illnesses that most adults would crumble under the pressure, these children are so resilient and keep on smiling despite the pain that they are in. The smiles that they give which just radiate energy for other people to be inspired is incredible. An amazing event, with great funds raised which contributed to reaching their target for little Nellie Rose to have overseas treatment in the United States which could potentially save her little life. Once again hope, faith and belief restored and love in such desperate times. The BEKS charitable organisation has done it again.

My lovely dear mother loved attending these events. She loved being there seeing her son doing something with his life. It made me feel blessed that my mother could witness my journey. My mother never really knew the extent of what I went through during my childhood due to the bullying and intimidation and sheer abuse that I received from my sister. This undoubtedly affected my later life stages, my character, my personality, my persona. It affected everything. My trust in women was zero, all down to one person whom I loved so much, despite all of that I loved her with all my heart, I was just a child. But I have been making changes in my life since the moment I changed my name. My journey changed and making changes psychologically can work. You just have to believe in the new page that you're starting the new chapter. I made changes to my path as I would have been either dead or back in prison - neither of those I needed or wanted. I did not wish to lead a negative life when you don't have to. We all have a choice: you have to listen and look for the signals and the signs as they are there. You just have to have faith and belief in yourself to make these changes.

Sadly, so many don't recognise the choices that are placed in front of them. The deterioration of their soul becomes beaten and with that many either end up homeless in prison or dead which is truly tragic when mental health issues beat you. This is a place I didn't want to end up in. I wanted my mother to be proud of her son and I would have so wished my father was alive to witness the success of my life. It's not about all the money in the world that you can own, it's about all the differences that you can make in other people's lives to make them feel better about their lives. This was the journey of BEKS.

During this time a very dear friend did something remarkably beautiful, and this was to do an interview with ITV Meridian news regarding nominating me for the Pride of Britain. This was something I truly didn't expect. My sister's son also nominated me for Pride of Britain which was a beautiful honour, to be recognised for something that you are doing for your community in helping others. What an honour to be considered and for even ITV to have me in their finals of the Pride of Britain Awards.

This for me was a smile and one that will stay with me until I close my eyes on this life, for people to nominate me for the good I have done for others, for the smiles that have been created in such times of despair. How beautiful of people to think of me! I absolutely love each and every one of them that took the time to consider me for a Pride of Britain award. I made the regional finals of Pride of Britain which was good enough for me. An amazing guy called Ben West went on to the main show in London and absolutely 'well done' to Ben for succeeding to be recognised for a Pride of Britain winner.

My mother witnessing herself on ITV Meridian news on my being recognised for a Pride of Britain nominee was beautiful for her and I'm so pleased she did. My lovely mother was proud. Life was treating me fairly. The charitable organisation was ticking along great, little projects forthcoming from taking elderly people out for a day down to the coast. And one in particular, a wonderful character, by the name of Ronald Brown. Ronald was 88 years old and an absolute character of life. Right away from meeting Ronald we had a connection. He kind of gave me back something I had lost, which was my father. I know my father could never be replaced but simply just to have someone to look up to and show love was magical.

Ronald was a character of life, he had already been on Blind Date on ITV along with Paul O'Grady. Ronald is an entertainer, he loves to sing and just be happy. Another tragic story came to me of a very young mother that had a serious disease and needed funds raised for treatment for her condition. Summer Barker was a young mum, a beautiful girl that was battling a disease which had to receive treatment in order for her to live a normal life to the best of her ability. With this I laid on another event which was a bus pull. To pull a bus as many times as I can to raise funds for the family of Summer Barker. I had the great privilege of Joe Egan to support and also the great privilege of another former professional boxer and actor that came to support me on the day, Scott Welch. Scott played a bare-knuckle fighter in the film 'Snatch' - what a lovely surprise for Scott to come and give support for my little event! This for me was a growing charitable organisation that was growing stronger with celebrity support gaining fast and that for me was showing I must have been doing something incredibly right. The event was a tremendous success and I met the beautiful family of Summer Barker and we all had t-shirts that made smiles and laughter and hope restored for a family that was battling challenges for their beautiful daughter.

The BEKS charitable organisation was growing strength to strength. I was very blessed to be introduced to a wonderful guy by the name of Mark McAllister. Mark ran a very successful business in London. Mark was a true angel and donated a beautiful little Nissan Pixo car for me to get about as the car that I was driving was literally falling apart. As I said I was a self-funded, non-profit organisation. I was financing the company from my own pocket and amazingly Mark McAllister surprised me with the beautiful little car for my charity which I had sign written, thanks to another amazing friend that has been a great support to the BEKS charitable organisation and that is Craig Dulieu. Craig runs a successful kitchen wrap company and vehicle wrapping company in Sittingbourne. I had the little BEKS car all sign written in the BEKS logos. I was really beginning to feel like I was taking my life into a new beautiful journey albeit some tears will be shed along its way but a tremendous amount of smiles will be made in the process. I could not thank Mark McAllister enough for his amazing support and the continuation of this support would be a tremendous strength to my little organisation.

I became extremely close friends with the family of the little Lyrah and continued to support and supply smiles for the family. Every time Lyrah used to see me she would run out and give me a big cuddle. This for me was priceless beyond words, truly priceless. We all became a very strong family, a unit of love and I would continue to give little birthday surprises which I did with two amazing friends of mine that dressed up as a princess from Frozen and another as another princess called Bella. There was a moment there on Little Lyrah's 9th birthday where I organised the two princesses to sing to Lyrah a beautiful tune along with the little princess dress that I bought for Lyrah to wear too and also feel like a magical princess.

This memory was one to stay with me for the rest of my eternal life. I used to think to myself the day that Lyrah wasn't here I would reflect back on these memories as an energy to step forward and keep going, creating these smiles for these amazing children that battle everyday and still smile. This was something I was witnessing even with adults that were battling stage four cancer and terminal illnesses, that an amazing depth of strength was brought to the surface where they would smile to you but the smile was always hidden by a world of pain. And this goes for people that suffer even with mental health issues. It's that mental health is not a scar that is visible, it's not something you can see and detect, it's something that's hidden behind the smile. Even those children as well as the adults battling terminal illnesses in some cases, to look at them you would think they are healthy and fine but in many cases behind those smiles are fears and those fears are of the day they lose their battle for life.

Lyrah gave me something back that I had lost. Lyrah captured something within my heart. Those beautiful drawings that she used to do for me, her pictures I had printed and put on my charity car. I wanted people to see the smile that Lyrah gave to me, of myself and Lyrah walking into the sunset. It was a magical drawing that meant so much and spoke volumes. The magical words that I lived by was to live, love and laugh and most of all, smile. I loved keeping in contact with all the families I had been supporting as I loved to hear the progress reports on their children as well as their lives, and that they were in a better place. That for me I knew my job was done successfully.

Rebecca's Legacy was living extremely strong. So many smiles had been made and so much hope and belief and faith restored in those that battled daily to even get out of bed and take a moment to walk when the strength to find the energy, when life, looked so dark.

Normally I would only fundraise or support families within the local Medway community, but there were some cases that I would step out and help. One was a family that lived in Birmingham, that had a little boy just aged 12 years old, also, with an inoperable brain tumour that needed a little help and support. And from that I could not walk away. Nicola, the mother, was an amazing lady, the whole family was an amazing family that was battling to smile for their little boy. They travelled to Kent for a little surprise that I had laid on for Daniel, to have a spin in a beautiful Ferrari which belonged to Mark McAllister and this was an experience any 12-year old boy would absolutely love. My dear friend Mark took Daniel for a spin and took the vehicle up to various speeds which brought a smile to Daniel which was a magical moment and once again for that short space of time Daniel forgot his fears and his worries. He just enjoyed the moment of that smile that was created in a super car Ferrari.

I began to gain a wealth of people that would do various smiles for these children. One of them was my dear friend, John, who owned a helicopter and with this also I made a date for Daniel to have a trip in my friend's helicopter over the coast of Dover in Kent. Two magical experiences and smiles made for a little lad that had his life cut short at the age of just 12 years. Daniel and his family became very close friends with Lyrah's family, Victoria and Lorna, and another family was made, another unit of strength, of network of people together, to support each other. The BEKS charitable organisation was not just simply and solely myself bringing smiles, it was bringing people together to support each other, families united as one, as a strength which was an amazingly beautiful thing to experience and witness. To network people together as one to support each other in similar circumstances was a great asset of strength.

The BEKS organisation had a varied age group which I supported. I took the elderly for trips out like Ronald Brown to Leysdown to play on the machines at the arcades. We would have breakfast and I would let Ronald sing to everybody which he truly loved to do.

Looking after the elderly is something that was very close to my heart as they become the forgotten people. After having contributed so much to society for so many years when you become old, you become forgotten, sitting in your home whilst alone, with just memories to keep you alive each day. Memories of what we have left towards the end of our lives. Regardless of age memories are eternal to the moment we close our eyes on this life, it's what we reflect back on. As they say your life flashes before you and if some of those flashes on moments of your life are laughter and smiles, then that is a blessing.

Life in general was blessed. I was managing to juggle the organisation as well as look after my mother and make sure her every need was catered for as I became my mother's primary carer. As we approached Christmas of 2020 I was slowly winding down as I wanted to make my mother's Christmas a truly special one. It had been a very busy year with many smiles made and I felt I needed a little break. I decided to take a few days away to adjust, to clear my head and recharge my batteries. I loved Folkestone. I had a deep passion for Folkestone. Every time I would take a trip to Folkestone I would take a big bunch of flowers to Molly Barker, the wonderful lady I did the Trishaw ride for. I always popped in to see her, to let her know she was being thought of. I decided to ask my sister's son to look after my mother for those few days away as I knew my mother loved his company and I knew he would not let me down and make sure my mother's medication was taken correctly.

During the day I explained how everything needed to be done to make sure everything was in place. We were just coming out of a Covid pandemic lockdown. Sadly, my mother never left the home. Her little legs were struggling to walk due to the lack of usage of the muscles in her legs. However, I bought her a walking frame so she could walk about the home comfortably which she did and was perfectly fine to make her breakfast in the morning and a cup of coffee which she did. She was a typical 82-year old lady but still managed to keep a little bit of her independence.

The long-awaited little break came for me and I decided to go away for a few days with my sister's son looking after my mother for just a few days. Some weeks before my sister and her son had suffered Covid. They both had the Covid virus. My sister's son had recovered from the virus. I had no contact with my sister at that time.

However, I was assured that my sister's son had recovered from the Covid so we had no fears regarding my mother catching Covid as I had protected her for two years during the pandemic. I sanitised my hands daily, washed everything, even the shopping was wiped down that I bought from time to time. Anything I brought into the home was sanitised. My mother's health was paramount; it was something I was very meticulous with, to detail.

I had a lovely few days away and loved every second of walking along the beach visiting the road of remembrance in Folkestone and just eating and relaxing and taking a little time out for myself which I so needed as I was physically and mentally drained as a lot of emotion is evolved in these cases and sometimes I need to reset my mind to go again. It was a beautiful, relaxed time. I thoroughly enjoyed my few days. I decided to drive home and was glad to be back with my mother and just take a little time to have a beautiful Christmas with her and make it memorable and fun and laugh. It was all I wanted to do - a little bit of family time or so needed after focussing on everyone and everything else for so long.

As I entered the front door of my mother's flat my mother looked asleep as I looked at her. She appeared half dressed in her petticoat and no skirt. This seemed extremely strange and something that I've never witnessed before. In all the years of my mother, she always got fully dressed before entering the living room. I said to my sister's son, why was my mother half dressed? He proceeded to say she had been a little bit strange the last few days. I asked if my mother's medication was given at the correct times as instructed and he assured me that this had been done. I checked the medication and it was correctly given throughout and administered properly through the blister packs as requested.

I then woke my mother to see how she was. My mother was acting extremely strange. Her speech was very slurred and her mannerisms were very slow. Something was not right, something did not seem right here and worry overtook me within seconds. My sister's son said he was going and left at that point. I thanked him for looking after my mother for those few days and I would take care of my mother from here on.

I proceeded to check my mother's medication in detail. With this I discovered a green and white capsule with FLX MIL. I had seen this tablet in my mother's medication over the last six weeks. I knew from time to time tablets would change shape and colour but would be still the same brand of tablet. This happened often, but I put my trust in the pharmacy to deliver the correct medication for my mother. I felt the need to Google this tablet to find out what it possibly could be as I realised it was something that had been in there over the last six weeks. Something was telling me to check and so I did and to my horror I discovered it was Fluoxetine 20 mg which was an antidepressant. I could not work out why my mother was taking antidepressants. This was something that was never prescribed for my mother and never should have been prescribed. I set out the following morning to see if this was something that had been prescribed without my knowing.

My mother was in a very delirious state, unable to communicate or talk to me. This was not the mother I had left some days before. Prior to this she was up and about, making her breakfast, making her coffee, talking and chatting normally. My neighbour, Steve, popped in to see my mother at the beginning when I went away and my mother seemed absolutely fine.

This was a serious concern to me as my mother's actions were not of the normal nature and had worried me incredibly, seeing her sitting there half-dressed and unable to eat or drink or communicate. The side effects of Fluoxetine indicated all these symptoms which my mother was showing and none of these were there prior to my going away.

The following day I telephoned doctors to check with them. I asked if they could run through the list of medications my mother had. The list showed there was no Fluoxetine ever prescribed. I asked the doctor if there was Fluoxetine at any one time prescribed for my mother and they said "no, no Fluoxetine has ever been issued or prescribed for your mother at any time." This was a serious concern. The doctors proceeded to tell me that it seemed to be a dispensary error from the pharmacy. And with this in mind I contacted the pharmacy to speak to the head pharmacist. I spoke to a lady on the phone and I also asked her if she could run through the list of medications on her computer. I wanted her to indicate to me what was on the list of medications. As the pharmacist went through the list indicating there was no Fluoxetine issued or prescribed for my mother, I explained my mother had been taking Fluoxetine for the last six weeks and was now on the sixth week.

The lady I spoke to on the phone who I assumed may have been the pharmacist, it turned out was one of the counter staff. I was asked to bring in the dosette boxes containing all the medications of the Fluoxetine. I said I would be in shortly to bring these medications to correct so I can minister my mother the correct medication.

I decided to take photos of all the boxes which the Fluoxetine was in. I needed evidence myself to show just in case my mother was taken seriously and have proof that the pharmacy had incorrectly given my mother Fluoxetine for a period of weeks which should not have been there. I also took a video of my mother in her delirious state and condition as a record to show the side effects were showing the same as indicated, which Fluoxetine would have given.

My mother's general health was not looking good at all. I took the Fluoxetine back to the pharmacy and I showed the head pharmacist what was in the dosette boxes and the head pharmacist proceeded to say to me, "I am extremely sorry for I got my "fs" mixed up. I should have given your mother for Furosemide 20 mg." This was a water retention tablet.

I said my mother was not in a very good state of mind. I was not happy with the results I got from the pharmacist. He seemed very relaxed in his attitude towards the serious mishap of getting his "fs" mixed up with medication that could potentially kill my mother. I decided to look into the side effects of other drugs that could not possibly mix with Fluoxetine and with further investigation I discovered Fluoxetine can cause gastrointestinal haemorrhage which means basically you could bleed from your oesophagus and your stomach. At this present moment in time I saw no signs of my mum losing any blood from her mouth; only her mental state was not in a great shape. However, my mother did show signs of recovery and seemed to be slowly getting better and with this I became a little more relaxed but made sure her medication was being administered correctly, like checking every conceivable tablet in great detail to make sure the pharmacist did not make any further errors as serious as this.

As a week or two passed, my mother wasn't really showing signs of a full recovery. She was sleeping a tremendous amount and not really being her normal self but I set the sights to give my mother a magical Christmas. My mother started to show signs of not eating properly but I made sure that our Christmas was going to be a magical one. And I invited my sister and her boyfriend to Christmas dinner so we could have a magical family day even though the way I felt about my sister was strong to the point I did not want her there but I did not want my mother to have a Christmas without her daughter. I pushed my feelings aside and made sure that Christmas day was a beautiful day and one that would stay with us all. A beautiful dinner was laid on, lots of silly hats, Christmas crackers, lots of food, lots of laughter, Christmas songs and Christmas presents for Christmas day. Everything could not have been any better. I made a great effort to set the table to look beautiful and special and one that made my mother smile. She was still not her normal self. I did have concerns but was hoping the effects of the Fluoxetine would eventually wear off and I would get my mother back to some kind of normality.

As the week progressed to New Year's Eve my mother still didn't seem any better. I telephoned the district nurse to come out and check my mother and just to make sure and give myself peace of mind that her blood pressure and statistics were all good. Our local district nurse came out and checked my mother over. Her blood pressure was reasonably ok, oxygen levels were a little low but not to the point of any concern. My mother's legs were suffering with swelling of fluid retention and cysts. I did explain to the district nurse the error of the pharmacy giving my mother Fluoxetine instead of Furosemide which is the correct medication for water retention, and the district nurse made sure that my mother's medication was also correct for my mother to receive the correct medication for her legs.

I made my mother as comfortable as I possibly could. I wanted her to have a beautiful Christmas but something was lurking deep inside my heart that was not giving me a great vibe. I was worried that this may be my mother's last Christmas. It was always a concern as my mother got older. My mother was my life, she is my life, she is my world, she is my entirety, she is the reason why I open my eyes every morning to life. The promise I made to my father whilst he lay dead in hospital, that I would look after his wife and my mother for the rest of her life, I still feel I failed that promise but towards the later years I made sure my mother had regular medical check-ups. I even made sure my mother received treatment for her neuralgia which we overcame by using chiropractors and acupuncture private healthcare which my dear friends, Anthony and Tracy, paid for.

Everything for my mother's health for the last five years to six years was paramount. I made sure my mother was catered for her health and life which was made comfortable at all times. My mother is my world and if I lost her I would lose me as a person because my purpose would be gone for eternal life and whether I would recover from that journey after getting and reaching my destination in my life where I should be, I was not sure I would recover from that loss. However, I lived in hope. I had lovely conversations with my mother prior to New Year's Eve where we sat and my mother would chat away telling me about her life. It was lovely, she told me how she used to work at the Grosvenor House Hotel in London and how hard she used to work when she came into this country in 1952.

She told me all about her life, how she lived it, how she met my father and how much she loved him and devoted her life to her husband, my beautiful father. She had spent longer away from him than she did, with him. My mother met my father in 1968 and my mother lost her husband in 1993 and sadly, my mother had spent over 30 years away from her husband, the love of her life. There was always a song my mother used to refer to that meant so much to her and that was 'Unchained Melody' from the amazing film 'Ghost'. Every time this song would be played my mother would look up at my father's photo on the wall in sadness. Beyond words, the look in my mother's eyes was a look that she just wanted to be with her husband again. She missed my father so much her heart was broken the day that my father sadly passed away. Over thirty years of loneliness for which I tried to make amends but I ended up in prison which only further damaged my mother's heart even more. When I look back over the years of my treatment to my mother I had broken her heart so many times for her to see me go to prison; shortly after losing her husband she also lost her son for a period of years. No matter what I did to make that better, it was very difficult and, sadly over the years, my sister along with everything and everyone I ever loved, set out to break that bond between myself and that person, and the poison that my sister fed my mother for so many years about me, regarding me, the use of steroids, the armed robbery, being accused of shooting people, 'your son is nothing but a spoilt horrible brat and has nothing to offer in life.' Along with my sister's long stretch of poisoning my mother's mind on me I knew I had my work cut out to see and show that I loved my mother in every way, shape or form. However, I lived with all that pain along with the treatment I gave my mother seeing her son go to prison. My sister was there poisoning her mind for decades. I really, truly didn't stand a chance but I was there in those last few years. The last several years of her life, I did not leave my mother's side and made sure her of healthcare and medication, her well-being, and to show love to her was paramount to me throughout those years.

However, things were about to change, and change in a way that was going to truly open up doors that I have feared all my life. Specifically, the last few years. The next chapter was one that was going to be a truly heart-breaking journey and one that I truly knew one day would come but not in such a brutal devastating heart-breaking way. Life was about to change for the worst.

⸻◆⸻

Chapter 14

Sons are the Anchors of a Mother's Life

O ver the last few weeks I had been battling my mother's ill-health. My mother's health had declined dramatically to the point of real concern for her life. The fear and desperation to see my mother back to her normal health was slipping away. Things were looking extremely serious. I put my mother to bed at approximately 11 p.m. on December the 30th 2020. My mother was in a very precarious condition; she most certainly was not her normal self in any way, shape or form. I took my mother to the bedroom and I then let my mother prepare herself for bed. This took a considerable amount of time, much more time than it would normally take for my mother to get herself into bed. I kept calling over, "Are you ok, Mum?" I very lightly got a response of "Ok".

Within myself I was struggling to cope and would often sit there and cry in desperation for my mother to recover from the medication that she was given by her pharmacy in error. Finally, my mother got herself into bed. I left the TV on in the bedroom for her, to help her get to sleep. My mother was struggling to breathe. After an hour or so I popped in to check on my mother and she had fallen asleep and seemed very restful. I then decided to pull my bed out which was a sofa bed in the living room and try and get some sleep myself, but during the night I would prepare myself to check on my mother just to see if she was ok.

During the night my mother would wake with a moaning sound at which I went to check on her, to see if she was ok. She seemed to be drifting in and out of sleep for the first few hours. Then after two or three hours my mum finally drifted off to sleep solidly and I finally fell asleep. I remember waking up around 6:15 a.m. I could hear my mother crying in pain. I stumbled out of the bed half asleep and ran to the bedroom just to check to see what the concern was. As I entered the bedroom, to my horror, I saw my mum lying extremely uncomfortably, as if she had tried to prop herself up in the bed but twisted. Something was certainly not right. My mum had been sick violently and I remember looking on the floor and there was a dark brown coffee granule looking vomit all over the floor and down the side of the bed and also down my mother's chest and side of her face. I panicked with regard to the dark brown coffee granule looking vomit all over the bed and floor and my mother.

I rushed to get my little blood pressure machine just to check my mother's blood pressure. On inspection it was incredibly low, seriously low. I then checked my mother's oxygen levels and they were barely 65 percent and dropping. I said to my mother, "I am going to have to call an ambulance. Her reply was, "Please babe, no, no, babe." I was in a panic state in shock. I waited a further 15 minutes and checked my mother's oxygen levels again and they had dropped below 50%. I then proceeded to say to my mother, "Mum I have to call an ambulance," and at that she reluctantly nodded.

The look in my mother's eyes was pure fear. My mother kept reaching out to hold my hand and the first time I missed her hand she could hardly hold her hand up at all. Her body had gone completely limp, her eyes were wide open. I've never seen eyes like this in my life. It was as if her pupils were huge and wide and the look of my mum within her eyes as she looked into my eyes, she knew this could be death. My beautiful mother's eyes, those eyes I will never forget, I've never seen that look in anyone's eyes in my life, the pure fear of death in my mother's eyes as she reached out to grab my hand for the second time. I held my mother's hand, and she looked at me with those eyes in pure fear that these may be her last minutes if not hours of her life.

I telephoned for the ambulance and waited for their arrival which took approximately 45 minutes. During those 45 minutes I held my mother's hand. All I could see around me was the brown vomit all down my mother's chest and floor and side of the bed. I was unsure what this was. My mother's breathing was extremely erratic as if trying to catch her breath, on every breath fighting for her life, fighting for her breath, eyes wide and getting wider as the fear became deeper.

I saw the ambulance approaching the front of the flat at around 8:30 a.m. New Year's Eve. Two female paramedics arrived at my mother's flat. The first response from one of the paramedics was, "Oh my god." Even the paramedic was in shock as to what she witnessed. I asked the paramedics, "What is that brown coloured vomit?" They both told me it looked like old blood which is normally coffee granules in colour.

This concerned me tremendously as deep within my thoughts the pharmaceutical error of Fluoxetine which was given to my mother mixed with Clopidogrel, about which when I Googled, these two drugs do not interact and don't work together. I had already investigated this and made a note. The two female Paramedics were absolutely shocked as to what they saw. My mother had urinated throughout the bed. The two paramedics cleaned my mother and managed to get her up on the bed. My mother looked up at the paramedics and blew them both a kiss. That was my mother, god bless her heart. She just wanted to say 'thank you'. She struggled to talk so she blew them both a kiss and both the paramedics said how lovely my mother was.

I found myself in a panic. I didn't know whether I was coming or going, or whether this was a nightmare. My anxiety and adrenaline, my fears, my sadness, my sorrow, my worry, everything was running through my mind and my heart was broken from witnessing my mother vomiting old blood. She obviously was bleeding internally and most likely for some time. I found my mother a little blouse which actually belonged to her sister, Zita, whom my mother sadly lost tragically in a road accident in 1987. I gave the beautiful blouse to my mother to wear whilst the paramedics were organising a wheelchair to take my mother.

I did not want my mother to go to hospital as my fear was I would never see her again. We were still dealing with a Covid pandemic and my fears were that I would not be able to sit with my mother. I needed to be beside her. I could not leave her side but I was told to stay put until the hospital telephoned me with any further updates. I saw my beautiful mother being wheeled away through the door and I looked through the living room window to see my little mother being wheeled into the ambulance as the doors closed. The silence in the flat was very daunting. I was left with a very strange silence of a mother that may not come back home.

Witnessing my mother covered in blood was not the vision I would have expected to ever see. To lose someone so beautiful in your life was a devastating thought. I understand we all have to leave this life on earth at some point but it's the way you leave this earth, a natural death is understandable. Everything was running through my mind. Was my mother going to die? Or was she going to be ok? Could the internal bleeding be kept under control and her breathing stabilised? I just didn't know anything at that time. Eventually the ambulance left to take my mother to hospital where she would be examined and I would know further on that day as to what the outcome would be.

I telephoned my sister with the news of our mother being rushed into hospital. She was proceeding to go to work that morning. She did genuinely seem very concerned for her mother and I explained once I knew further updates from the hospital I would telephone her to let her know. As the morning went on, the silence in the flat was unbearable. I really struggled with the emptiness. The void was too upsetting. I telephoned my very close friend, Clint, and told him the situation as I cried to him on the phone. He said he would come and pick me up and take me for a little bit of breakfast and for that I said, "Thank you so much." I needed a friend at that moment in time. My heart and soul had taken a beating. The vision would not leave my mind, what I witnessed of her being covered in blood.

Clint picked me up and took me to a McDonald's just to get me out of the flat. Whilst I was with him the hospital telephoned me with an update. I believe it to be a nurse that I spoke to. She proceeded to tell me that my mother had a chest infection and was now being treated with antibiotics. The nurse also told me that they had stabilised my mother's breathing and she was stable at present. I suddenly relaxed to the thought of 'thank god it's just a chest infection'. I was elated albeit my mother was in hospital but she was not dying. The relief within my soul was of pure elation as my mother would be coming home in a day or two and I would get her well again like I did last time to get her back on track and get rid of the chest infection that my mother had accumulated. I was told that they had done a Covid test and were awaiting the results.

I telephoned my sister straight away and told her, "It's ok, mother has just a chest infection and she is being treated with antibiotics." With that my sister was relieved. I could tell of her concerns on the phone. I proceeded to tell her that they had done a Covid test and were awaiting the results. However, my mother was stable and it was just a chest infection. Both of us we were truly relieved just hearing my mother had something that was treatable. I explained to my sister, any further news I would let her know.

An hour and a half had passed. I had eaten my McDonald's with Clint and he was going to take me back home. As we were driving out of McDonald's I received another telephone call from the hospital. This time it was a consultant. The consultant proceeded to tell me my mother's condition had dramatically deteriorated and there had been signs of further coffee granule blood from my mother's mouth. It was then explained to me by the consultant that due to my mother's condition deteriorating, my mother approximately had maybe one hour or two hours to live. For a few seconds whilst on the phone with the consultant, those seconds felt like eternity. I didn't believe what I had just heard. I could not take in the words 'one to two hours to live'. Only a couple of hours ago I was told my mother just had a chest infection and now she was dying.

How could this be? How could this change so dramatically in just two hours? I went from being elated to having my mother home to my mother never coming home. The consultant explained to me that if I wished to attend the hospital they would grant me permission to be beside her. I said I would be there right away. I looked around at Clint and I could see tears in his eyes. He said he would take me to the hospital. I then telephoned my sister to tell her the tragic news. I explained to my sister, "I think it's best you come to the hospital as Mum has only hours to live." My sister burst into tears on the phone and said, "How is this possible? It was just a chest infection." I explained that her condition had seriously deteriorated in a short space of time and now time was very limited for mother. I explained that I was on the way to the hospital and I would meet her there. Clint took me to the hospital and we found the ward that my mother was in, which was the Sapphire ward at Medway Hospital. On arrival at the hospital I spoke to reception staff and explained I was there to see my mother. I was given a mask, gloves and gown to wear. I was then escorted to my mother. As they pulled the curtain back I could see my mother and this was a vision that would also never leave me. It was explained to me by a consultant that I would agree to not resuscitate. This was a decision to end my mother's life and not revive her. Signing my mother's leaving of this world without a fight, without trying - how could I sign a document for my mother to die? I had to make that decision for my mother not to be resuscitated. This is something I never would have expected to do in my entire life, to waiver my mother's life by a signature, to let her die.

I looked over at my mother, in tears, crying. Clint was still there with me. I could also see tears in his eyes. I was so blessed with such a genuine, true friend that stood beside me at my mother's point of death. I was truly blessed with such a loyal, true friend. He is my brother and I will never forget his support for me as my mother left this world.

My sister finally arrived and Clinton decided to go. He gave me a cuddle and said, "Call me when you need me." I struggled to find any words to say other than, "Thank you and I will call you as soon as I can." I pulled up a chair beside my mother and I stroked her hair. I kissed her forehead and said, "I love you Mum, I love you so much please don't go." My sister stood at the front of the bed and just looked on. Deep within my heart and soul I knew this was the end and for me to decide to sign a 'do not resuscitate' was one of the toughest things I've ever had to do, to kiss goodbye to my mother's life on my decision to say 'do not resuscitate', which I agreed to with a consultant, as part of my soul knew my mother was yearning for her husband, to be back together again. Something within my heart was telling me it was time for my mother to leave this world to go to heaven and meet all her beautiful family that she had lost over the years - her brothers and sisters and mother and, of course, her devoted husband and my beautiful father -for her to be all together again. My heart was broken. I agreed to not resuscitate.

My mother's breathing was extremely erratic. She looked peaceful but that was due to the high levels of morphine that my mother was injected with. My mother was still losing blood from her mouth. The nurse returned to inject my mother's stomach again with morphine. My mother cringed and raised her legs. Obviously, she could still feel pain. She slightly opened her eyes but only for seconds. I continuously kept stroking her hair and told her I loved her as I held her hand and the nurse proceeded to suck the remainder of the old blood from my mother's mouth and I could see my mother's tongue trying to battle the suction tool in her mouth.

As the nurse left I still sat there holding my mother's hand, leaning over her, crying, and in pure devastation that this could not be happening. All of sudden my mother started to kick her legs and shake her head from side to side as if to say, 'No I'm not going, I'm not ready to go.' Part of me was thinking the other side of the spirit world was now pushing my mother to leave and she may have seen somebody there calling her that she didn't want to be called by. That was my perception at that moment. She then relaxed and calmed down. Another nurse came and said, "Would you like us to take you to a room where you can be in private with your mother?" I agreed and said that would be fine.

As my mother was wheeled into a private room where myself and my sister could sit with her, my sister remained standing at the front of the bed whilst I sat beside my mother holding her hand and kissing her face telling her I loved her. Deep within my heart I was saying sorry for the son I'd been. I hadn't been a great son, nothing for her to be proud of as she left this world. I was a disappointment as a son. I believe that within my heart.

151

My mother's breathing became slower and slower as if there were a few seconds' gaps in between each breath. I could tell her heart rate was slowing down and was nearing the end after 82 years of life. Suddenly it was gone, with 52 years of the most beautifullest woman in the world that brought me into this world, carried me for nine months, looked after me for all those years, and towards the end of her years I became her carer, as the tables had turned.

My mother's breathing got slower and slower to the point I could see the last breath was coming and then she was gone. I could not see a further breath taken. I could not see any further signs of life as my mother's cheeks of her face started to drop and the circulation in her body had stopped. My mother had died. There was pure silence in the room as myself and my sister cried. Devastation is a word that doesn't even come close to how we both felt even though the way I felt about my sister was of pure hate. At the end of the day it was still her mother. I had to respect that and felt sorry for her loss as her mother too had died.

A thousand thoughts running through my mind, I held my mother's hand again and stroked her hair as the tears ran down my face onto her cheek. The loss was truly soul wrenching. It was as if the devil had grabbed my soul, held it in his hands and threw it to disregard its worth. I became empty that very second. It was as if the umbilical cord of a spiritual connection between myself and my mother had been cut. Part of me died that very minute. My only consoling thoughts in all this twisted moment in time was that my father, my beautiful dad, had called my mother. After over 30 years of loss they are back together again. I could see the colour in my mother's face changing and on her arms as the blood circulation had stopped. I could see the change and I feared this change in many ways, the closing of a chapter of a part of my life I was never going to see again but only have memories.

I remember standing up and just looking at my mother. So, this is life, so this is the ending of a chapter of a small moment in time called life, the discovery of how fragile life truly is, is beyond any conception of understanding of its worth. My sister was in pure shock and hardly said any words at all. Of course, there came a point that we had to leave the hospital as the nurse had double checked my mother's pulse and my mother was confirmed dead at 6:20 p.m. on the 31st of December 2020. This was exactly the same time, 6:20 p.m., that my father had passed away as his retirement clock stopped at 6:20 p.m. and his wrist watch stopped at 6:20 p.m. which he was wearing the day he died and my mother passed away at 6:20 p.m.

We were left for a period of time just to say our farewells. I gave my sister a hug and held her tight. This was her mother too and I felt her sorrow. The hardest part is when you have to walk away from your loved one as they lay dead in front of you knowing that was the last physical vision that you will see of your loved one. As we proceeded to leave the room I remember kissing my mother, stroking her hair again and telling her, "I love you, Mum. Until we meet again, God bless you." I said the Lord's Prayer in my mind and may she be blessed in God's heaven with all her loved ones and rest in peace with her beautiful husband, my wonderful father.

As I got to the door to leave the room I remember looking around at my mother. This was the last physical vision I would ever have in my entire life. There was numbness within my heart and my soul was dead. My soul had died and part of my soul had gone forever; nobody can explain that feeling until it happens to them but part of my soul had left this earth too. I held the door for a few seconds in my hands as I walked out from the room. I remember the door closing as I slowly walked away looking back at my mother lying on the hospital bed, just her shell, the carrier of her soul was lying there. I knew my mother's spirit would be around that room hovering wherever it might have been. I knew she could see me.

As the door started to close eventually my vision of my mother was limited and the door closed. As I walked away the strange feeling of leaving your world in a room, your life, your entirety, your soul, your love - it just felt odd, wrong how could you just leave your loved one in a room? After 52 years of being in my life it's now gone forever. There is no return, my mother's eyes won't see me no more, her life is gone.

As I walked away I battled my tears as well as my sister, to not gather my thoughts to any kind of adjustment to what had just happened. We telephoned our cousin to pick us up from the hospital and take us home. We left the reception area of the hospital and I waited for our lift for our cousin to take us back home. Obviously, our cousin was devastated by the news of the loss of his auntie. The silence within the car was of emptiness.

I was dropped back home to be left on my own whilst my sister was taken home by my cousin. I remember walking in the door of my mother's flat to be left with the silence and the strange feeling of emptiness, loneliness and the void, the massive empty dark hole of a void. I remember sitting down and just simply listening to the silence where I would never hear my mother's voice again, I would never see my mother sitting in her armchair ever again. My mind was off memories. I cried tremendously as this was the rest of my life, another chapter I will have to battle and very much most likely on my own as I always have done.

The loss of a mother is the most devastating thing any person could ever feel. When you are born you have a lifeline called the umbilical cord to your mother and once that is cut life is down to you, and you, solely, to live. Once you lose a mother your lifeline is cut again but this time there is no reason for you to live. As a baby you yearn for your mother's connection, when you lose that and there is no connection or bonding and it's been taken away, then part of your soul also is taken away. On the 31st of December 2020 New Year's Eve, I heard fireworks in the sky, and people celebrating, people laughing in the streets. I could hear outside the window screaming of joy and happiness of a celebration of the new year of 2021. The fireworks were a continuation of celebration as I sat in the silence of an empty heart that had no reason for celebration. The 1st of January 2021 was the first day of the rest of my life in a new chapter. This new journey of this chapter was going to be one that would be very daunting. As the celebrations slowed throughout the early hours I still remained awake.

Where does one go from here? The thought of organising a funeral was far away. I could not accept the fact my mother was dead. I had spent all evening and the early hours alone crying on my own, dealing with the death of my mother on my own, but this was always my destiny, to be on my own. I have dealt with everything in life on my own and I was about to deal with my mother's death on my own.

The next stage of this journey was one that would break me totally as I knew the forthcoming weeks were going to be extremely painful. I failed to sleep at all and proceeded to head to the local corner shop to buy alcohol with a view to drown my sorrows in drink. I have never been a drinker and never liked alcohol at all but I needed something to take me away from the reality which I was in. I said so many prayers, I cried so many tears as I held my mother's cardigan. I had to find the energy but I failed to do so and continued to drink throughout the morning until my sister finally came around to discuss the situation at hand.

The next part of this journey is one that was also going to leave me scarred for the rest of my eternal life and I knew the devil had grabbed me once again for his joy to destroy my soul after my taking so much time and effort to heal the wounds of my life to that very point I'd reached. I felt I had reached my goal in life, of happiness, and just as I reached and touched my finding of this life it was swiftly taken away. I realised further how fragile life truly is. My world had ended completely. My purpose was my mother. My mother was my reason why my eyes opened up everyday day. My mother was my entirety and now the purpose was gone eternally.

Chapter 15

The Devil came for me Again

As the hours and days were passing, the darkness and realization of the loss of my mother was sinking in. My mother still lay in the mortuary of Medway Hospital. I kept thinking of her lying there – cold, alone, it was just a shell, the carrier of her soul - but the thought of her lying there was heart-breaking when she should be at home sitting in her armchair drinking her coffee and laughing and joking with me. I was taking regular trips to the corner shop and buying large amounts of alcohol. I was drinking excessively heavy, breakfast through lunch, and throughout the evening and the night, my drinking was excessive. I was not eating any food, I could not eat. My stomach would not take any food and I had no hunger at all. I constantly cried. My memories of my mother, the happy times, flashbacks to my childhood of my mother taking me to school, holding my hand - it was now apparent that memories were all I was going to have of my mother and her time with me over the 52 years of my life.

I had little or no sleep at all but I had to find strength as I wanted to fight for justice for my mother for what the pharmacy had done by giving her Fluoxetine instead of Furosemide along with the mixture of Clopidogrel which caused my mother to bleed internally. The paramedics confirmed that the coffee granules blood that they witnessed on the floor was old blood which indicated my mother had suffered internal bleeding of some kind.

My sister did take the time to come and sit with me most days which was comforting at that moment in time. Friends were very comforting to bring me food around to make sure I had eaten and making sure that I was ok. I spent hours on my own, specially, on an evening I would drink even heavier to numb the pain I was feeling inside.

Within days of my mother's passing, Medway Hospital telephoned me to confirm my mother tested positive for Covid-19. I could not understand how my mother would have caught Covid. I had not even had a cold, nothing. I had no signs of any infection or virus or anything. I knew it could not have been me. I knew my sister had had Covid some weeks before but to my knowledge my sister never came around to see my mother during the time of her isolation. My sister's son looked after my mother during the few days that I was away and some weeks previously he had also had Covid but to my knowledge he had been weeks clear. So, all in all, I could not work out how it was possible my mother would have had Covid. My mother showed no signs of Covid. She always had a cough but that was her COPD. My mother had no temperature at any time as I checked it regularly. Even when the district nurse came to check my mother over there were no signs of Covid. This seriously confused me.

I decided to open my laptop and start making moves towards approaching the General Pharmaceutical Council with a view to have an investigation to be placed into the pharmacy that gave my mother Fluoxetine by error. I also wished for a post mortem to be carried out to determine if Covid was apparent on my mother's lungs. I needed to clear that from my mind and work on the fact that my mother died as a result of the incorrect medication that was given to her.

Fighting for my mother's case was the cause to keep strong. I had no choice as I had no help. I had to fight for justice for my mother, and to determine the reason why she had been bleeding internally. I needed a post mortem to be carried out. I needed to determine the actual cause of death. The anger inside me was fierce. I kept away from people for fear of losing my temper and a world of anger spinning out on a victim. I did not want to subject anybody to that so I kept myself to myself and continued to drink excessively - daily, hourly, nightly. I did not stop drinking.

The darkness in my soul was becoming cold with every demon and devil pulling at what was left of a beaten soul that could not take anymore. My drinking was not working. My sister decided I should use another form of relaxant, drugs. My sister suggested weed. I have never used it before but I immediately said, "Yes, I will have it. I will buy a few bags whatever form it comes in." I struggled smoking the weed as I had never smoked before but it felt like it was helping so I bought more from my sister.

On January the 13th 2021 I decided I wanted to end my life. I could not take the painful journey ahead. I could not cope with my purpose; my reason and my entirety were now gone. There was nothing more for me to live for, my reason for life was gone. I was at the end of my road, a road that had no direction, there was no left turning, there was no right turning and there was no ahead; it was a dead end and one I couldn't walk backwards on as the damage of my past was too intense. I could not cope.

I had already considered taking my life when I came out of prison. It was a very close encounter to closing my eyes on this world but this time it was very different. The feeling was mentally powerful and overwhelming. Powerful to the point of no return. There was no preparation, there was no letter written, there were no farewells. I was just a desperate man in a desperate place. There was no light at the end of my tunnel. I wanted to leave this world and be with my mother and my father and live the happy times we used to have.

Flashbacks of my childhood would come into my mind of one particular sunny day whilst in a garden in her old home. The sun was shining. My beautiful dog, Blackie, was running around happily, my auntie Rose sitting there chatting away with my mother and my father cooking sausages on a barbecue. I was 14 years old in this flashback. I had just started weight training to feel I was a strong soul. The flashback continued to myself smiling happily with the contentment of my surroundings and how beautiful and happy that moment truly was.

I'd worked so hard to make my mother proud for those last few years. It was my objective for her to see her son successful at something in his life, something that made me happy every day to wake up with a purpose, yet that purpose and everything surrounding it had been taken away. I had become my mother's primary carer for the last 12 months of her life where I daily catered to her needs. She was very capable of making her own breakfast and coffee, she was the typical 82- year old. She would pop down to the high street twice a week and do a little shopping prior to the pandemic but the Covid pandemic destroyed my mother's confidence to walk outside the front door.

My mother's legs became excessively swollen with water retention hence why the doctors prescribed my mother Furosemide to keep the water retention under control on her legs. My goal was to get my mother back out shopping again, and live a sensible life but this had diminished due to the Covid pandemic. My mother had lost all her confidence which hindered her mobility, of using her legs, which she didn't do for almost a year and a half.

I had tried to the best of my ability and I felt that I had failed. If I had seen these tablets sooner could I have prevented my mother from dying? All the ifs, buts and maybes ran through my mind which were destroying me even more. The time was approaching 2:30 a.m. January 13th. I decided to eat all the weed cakes my sister had made, there must have been at least eight which were packed with weed.

I then decided to drink excessive amounts of alcohol and with that I grabbed the remainder of what was in the bag and decided to eat it all and various other forms of medication to swallow.

I became very unsettled, delirious and shaky. I remembered sitting in the armchair dreaming of my mother, of the happy times we had. I started to shiver. I felt extremely cold but I thought this was my mother coming to get me. She had come to collect me, to take me to a happy place away from this world of hurt. I wanted to leave this place and head for a better world of peace, tranquillity and love with the people I called my family.

As I was shivering I was talking to my mother out loud, "Mum I know you're here. I can feel you. I know you're here. I can feel you." I swallowed more weed and drank more alcohol so I could just simply shut my eyes and drift away into the new world. Suddenly I felt my tongue twisting in my mouth to the back of my throat. I then felt my chest tighten and I became breathless. I could not focus. I was shivering in the ice cold. I realised this possibly could be the point of death if I was about to die. I then started to panic and changed my mind. I didn't want to die. It was not my time to go, then the fear kicked in. I believed I was having a heart attack. My tongue was at the back of my throat.

I then stumbled up off the armchair to grab my phone to call for an ambulance. I could hardly talk and my hands were shaking and my vision was blurred. I realised if I had passed out no one would have known. I would have been here for days. I seemed to find the strength to call 999 for an ambulance which seemed to take eternity. I managed to talk to the operator and asked for an ambulance. I then proceeded to tell the operator I believed I was having a heart attack. After taking various details an ambulance was to be sent out to me.

I struggled giving information to the operator. She could hear I was in a panic state and struggling to talk, with my chest tightening excessively. I truly thought at that moment I was going to die. My mind was not in a good place. Finally, the ambulance pulled up and I kissed my little cat, Poppy, goodbye, just in case I never returned.

The ambulance pulled in the exact same position and place like only a week and a half previously. My mother was taken to hospital from the same spot. I truly believed this was the end of my life. I was so far out of my head on drugs and drink. I could not focus on reality in any way, shape or form. As I was put into the ambulance the paramedics placed something in my left arm into my vein and took my blood pressure and oxygen levels, of which the paramedics spoke to each other. This was a serious condition. My heart rate was through the roof and my blood pressure was at breaking point and at that point, I remember passing out.

Did I see any bright lights of another world? No. But I remembered becoming conscious again in the ambulance and the paramedic saying, "We may have to take you to Ashford accident and emergency as there is no room at Medway Hospital." With this I did not know where I was. I didn't know who I was anymore. I remember being taken into a hospital and placed in the accident and emergency area to my knowledge.

I was still half conscious. All I can remember was bags of a watery solution above me along with tubes and wires. I remember a nurse in my blurred vision placing two probes onto my chest and further probes around my chest. I came in and out of consciousness from time to time. I remember turning to my right and looking at the cabinets and remember seeing the words "resuscitation unit". I knew this was serious. A nurse then proceeded to place, what looked like to me, an extremely long thin wire into a vein in my left arm and it looked like it had a little tiny probe on the end that was placed into my vein.

I was still struggling with consciousness and remember the nurses running around me. I can remember the machine that was monitoring my heart rate was buzzing in the red zone from time to time. I can remember hearing the buzzing noise. Further realisation came to me, but comforting in a way, that my mother was under the same roof as me. My dear mother was still in the mortuary at Medway Hospital and I was only corridors away from her and even still at that point I was not sure if I was going to be next to her that night. I still wasn't sure if I had had a heart attack or whether I was going to pull through. I just did not know. But what I did know was, I was near my mother. She was close to me. We were under the same roof. It felt strangely comforting and warming to know I was near my mother again.

Something within me was fighting. I can't tell you what that was. I had no idea but my job wasn't done on this earth. Two, maybe three, bags of the clear fluid solution were pumped into me and I managed to somehow gain consciousness. One of the doctors was saying to me, "Are you a diabetic?" I proceeded to say 'no'. I never gave the doctors or nurses or consultants any indication that I tried to take my life. I never told them what I had taken or what I'd been drinking. I kept that to myself. I suddenly needed to go to the toilet desperately but I couldn't so they passed me a small bottle to use. It appeared that the more of the solution they were pumping into me the more I felt conscious. It was explained to me by one of the consultants that I was severely dehydrated which was extremely dangerous. I was still in a very dazed, delirious state of mind. I had swallowed a large amount of weed, a drug I had never used before and a large amount of alcohol and tablets. I was still very unsteady and extremely weary. I suddenly had a big x-ray machine placed in front of my chest and was told to breathe in and out. Somewhere close by I could hear a machine and monitor. It sounded like my heart was beating extremely fast but I could hear it. The room surrounding me was extremely quiet. It was not busy. I appeared to be the only one in there. I clearly remember I could hear my heart beating on a screen or monitor.

I came to realise that my attempt on taking my life was extremely half-hearted. Part of me wanted to go and part of me wanted to stay to fight for justice for my mother as I would believe my mother wouldn't want me to go this way. Suddenly some hours later two nurses walked up to me. They said nothing at all to me. They clipped the wires from my left arm, pulled the thin wire away from me and unplugged the wires off my chest, pulled my t-shirt down and nodded to me, "You can go now." The silence of the room felt extremely eerie. The whole moment felt strange bearing in mind my mother was in the mortuary. All these feelings and emotions were running through my mind.

Two nurses simply said, "You can go now." That very moment I believed I had died, that very moment I believed I had passed away. I didn't feel anything. In fact, I felt a peace. I felt calm. I felt very weary and was not sure about what had just happened. I stood up and nobody said anything to me, nobody. No consultant, no doctor, nobody came up to me to tell me what had happened. I was just told to go, it was my time to go. "You can go home now." I remember standing up but I refused to look round at the bed in case I saw my body still lying there which would have confirmed that I had actually died. I did not want to turn around to see my corpse. This particular moment in time was my death. I walked out of the ward towards the big double doors and could hear a mumbled voice behind me. I still refused to turn around to look, in case I saw myself on the bed which would have confirmed I had actually gone. Part of my soul was accepting death and part of my soul was saying I was alive but refused to look to see if I was truly dead.

I walked towards the double doors and opened them up to walk out. I had no idea where I was going. My head was spinning. I was still very dizzy and unsteady on my legs. I remembered walking to the accident and emergency area. It was almost daylight outside. I obviously must have been in there for some hours. I had no concept of time but I remember walking towards the telephone area to telephone for a taxi home. As I reached the telephone I picked the receiver up to call the number on the phone to dial for a taxi and the telephone number was 01634 666 666. This was surely confirmation I was going to hell for being the horrible little boy that I was told I was for so many years. I strongly believed I was going to hell. I was telephoning the devil to take me to his depths of darkness where I belonged. The telephone number 666 666 indicated the devil and I was on my way to hell.

I telephoned for a taxi and spoke to a very normal person on the other end of the phone who ordered my taxi. I was told my taxi would be approximately 15 to 20 minutes. I was still unsure if this was the other world that I was in and this is how nobody actually left earth. The spirit would just hover on earth and feel peace and tranquillity which I was feeling. I didn't feel ill, I felt calm. I believed I was heading for a very dark place but strangely felt fine.

As the taxi pulled up outside, I saw it was a white taxi. I remember jumping in the back and asking the driver to take me to my home. The silence in the car was still hard. I still believe the taxi was taking me to hell. I was in a tremendously strange, relaxed state accepting the fact I was going to hell because I believed how bad I truly was. As the taxi approached home, I paid the taxi driver with the remainder of money I had in my pocket. I remember being dropped off at home and walking indoors to my flat and believed even still that it was my spirit that came back to the flat just to say goodbye whilst a taxi waited outside for me to take my soul back to the devil.

I remember sitting down stroking my lovely cat and slowly, but surely, I began to realise it was the drugs that I had consumed along with the alcohol and everything else with it that made me believe I was dead. I made a cup of tea and thought I would telephone my sister to give her an update on me and test if I was actually alive for real.

The confirmation of the telephone told me I was actually still alive. It was the drugs and drink that I had consumed heavily that had made me feel delirious and believe I was dead. In its strange entirety it was a serious kick of reality that if you play with death it may just take you but something kept me from leaving this earth. There was a purpose for me to serve and that was to obtain justice for my mother and keep the promise I made to my father, even though my mother was not here any longer but to maintain the promise and fight for my mother. I had a second chance again.

Mentally I was in a very dark place. I was very blessed with beautiful friends. I explained to Clint what had happened I told very few people of my experience of what I believed was the end of my life. From that moment on I was not going to drink anymore alcohol or take any drugs ever again. This was my second escape from taking excessive amounts of drugs. This was my third escape of almost taking my life and two intended suicide attempts. My chances were running out and I may not be so lucky the next time.

I proceeded to fight for justice for my mother and was hourly and daily sending emails to the General Pharmaceutical Council and also to the head of the pharmacy. Then I was dealing with the post-mortem as my mother's body would not be released until a post mortem had been carried out as I had demanded an investigation into my mother's death to obtain the cause of death and to proceed with an inquest for my mother. The issue that I had was of a positive test for Covid-19, but this didn't deter the investigation which was desperately needed. I still occasionally drank but it was minimal. Some days it was more than others but I stayed away from the drugs.

A post-mortem date was set and the thought of my mother being cut open was extremely upsetting but I had to find out the cause of death. My strong beliefs were that the mixture of Fluoxetine and Clopidogrel was the cause of my mother's death. It was explained to me by the coroner that the paramedics witnessed brown coffee granule vomit which was confirmed to be old blood. These were primary side effects of such drugs that if mixed do not work together or interact in any way. I simply Googled all the drugs in question that my mother was taking to indicate what did not mix with Fluoxetine and it appeared Clopidogrel was one of them that did not interact. I then received the telephone call that was further to break my heart even more. Lyrah's mother, Victoria, telephoned me to tell me that Lyrah was dying. How could this be so soon after my mother? Losing such a beautiful soul, a 9-year old little girl, about whom we all knew at some point the brain tumour could not be kept at bay, but to be told the words that little Lyrah was battling for her last breath was beyond any thoughts that any mind could ever think of. I knew I had to be beside her to hold her hand in the final moments of her life. I had to gain strength. I could not let that little girl down that was always so excited to see me, do drawings for me, which I had put on my car. That meant so much to me, I had to be there for her. I drove immediately to Faversham with so many thoughts running through my mind. My heart was breaking and I knew the mother, how she must have felt losing her beautiful daughter. I truly understood the loss and the devastation that such a loss could do to your heart and soul.

I finally arrived at Faversham where Lorna, Victoria's mum, walked me through to Lyrah in the living room as she lay on the bed which the hospital had supplied for her. With Lyrah was the small fluffy, bunny rabbit called Hoppity that Lyrah had named. Lyrah took the bunny everywhere with her when she had chemo, on every hospital visit. Everywhere that Lyrah went, so did Hoppity. I'm so glad that the little bunny that I gave her, gave her warmth, love and kindness. Something so simple can mean so much and so beautiful.

I remember sitting beside Lyrah and I grabbed her little hand and held it in my hand. I was left alone with Lyrah while I said my final words that, "Rocky loves you and I will always love you and I promise I will always be here for you and I will not leave your family's side. I promise you. God bless you, beautiful princess Lyrah, God bless your soul, darling, I love you."

This was a 9-year-old little girl that did not even have the chance to enjoy life, become a teenager, find love, get married, have children, live a normal life. This little girl was not given the chance. I then questioned God, I questioned Jesus and Mother Mary, the almighty God, "Why are you taking this little girl away from her mother?" I questioned faith and everything about it. Why do this to a little girl that has done nothing to harm anybody? Yet you have made her suffer in pain with endless chemotherapy, injections, everything - the pain this little girl has gone through and yet she still smiled every day.

I held Lyrah's little hand and as she battled for her last breath, the erratic breathing was exactly the same as my mother's. Just a couple of weeks previously I was holding my mother's hand the same way saying goodbye. I was trying to understand the purpose of life, the fragility of life. I could not understand its purpose and its reasons. It's times like these that you question life. Everything I've ever loved and cared for, leaves me. I loved little Lyrah like my own daughter. Lyrah gave me something back that I'd lost, something so special and beautiful that I embraced. Every time she put her little arms around me, she made me feel like a special person and made me smile.

I thought in my own mind of the little special occasions I did for Lyrah. I had two princesses. I had them all dressed up for her to sing to her 'happy birthday' with a surprise stretch limo. The trip to Hamleys. All those little memories made, captured as photos in my mind, that will be there until my dying day. The way I see that particular moment in time was just days before, when I believed I was dead in hospital, high on drugs and alcohol. It wasn't my time. I could not leave this earth without holding Lyrah's hand and the angels, the Gods, whatever, was picking me up off the floor of my depths of darkness. I was not meant to leave this world until I completed my job on earth and looking at little Lyrah, I realised my purpose and that was -making people smile. It was something that I truly loved to do. Nobody understood the reasons why I did the things I had done, but when you see a 9-year old little girl smile as a result of something very simple - giving a small floppy bunny rabbit which Lyrah called Hoppity. She treasured that bunny and loved that bunny and would never let it go until the point when she took her last breath with Hoppity still in her arms.

I came away that day, extremely broken. Only a couple of weeks previously, I had lost my beautiful mother, holding her hand as she slipped away into the next world, and then the next moment I'm holding a 9-year old's little hand as she slipped away too. I strongly believe there is something we all go to, I believe there is another world that awaits us, I believe that everything happens for a reason but I could not get to grips why if there was a God that we all pray to, why does he take a 9-year-old little girl that has done no harm to nobody? I struggled with that concept of life.

I held Victoria and Lorna close and the family, and told them, "I am here, I am not leaving your side." I drove back home in absolute tears.

I learnt a lot about life in the space of just a couple of weeks and that is how fragile our existence truly is. None of us know what tomorrow brings. None of us can determine the future. I also realised that life is what you make it. You have to live happily and fight for what you believe in and never give up on your dreams no matter what it takes to get there. You have to live your life the way you want to live it. At the moment we close our eyes on this life you have to be content with your journey. I knew it was not my mother's time to go and looked at little 9-year old Lyrah's life and said to myself that was not her time to go, but we can't determine tomorrow; it's out of our hands.

Two funerals lay ahead of me, one of my mother's, and one of Lyrah. I was not sure how I was going to cope or even if I was going to pull through. I still wasn't eating regularly. I had lost a tremendous amount of weight. I was still in shock. So, what is this life all about? I kept questioning my existence but had to keep strong to fight for a case for my mother and to gain an inquest date into her death once the post mortem reports came back, which would give some indication to a direction for inquest.

I had a lot of time to think on my own, and came to the conclusion, that once my mother was buried and laid to rest, I would close doors on certain people in my life. Those that have done me damage and those that set out to hurt me and this was my sister. I had worked this out many years before when my father was laid to rest, when my sister said to me, "I have never loved you as a brother," in her drugged and drunken state. I had always said to myself, once my mother was laid to rest I would close the door on my sister and all her family for eternal life.

From somewhere I gained strength. I still was drinking occasionally just to take the edge off my feelings but I had to gain strength. The inquest was to gain justice for my mother. This was my primary goal but during this time we had to wait until the post-mortem had been done of which I finally got the results. My mother's primary cause of death was gastrointestinal haemorrhage of the oesophagus and stomach, secondary cause was heart disease and lung disease. This confirmed my suspicions that my mother had died as a result of the medication that was given in error by the pharmacy. With this

I could now fix a funeral date for my mother for which my mother's body could be released from the mortuary in Medway Hospital, to be taken to the funeral directors upon a date which was set for February the 11th, 2021.

Chapter 16

Laying your Demons to Rest

My mother was finally taken to the funeral directors which was literally across the road from where I live. Nightly I would walk past the funeral directors and say a prayer to my mother and blow her a kiss and tell her I loved her. There was heavy snow on the ground. It was freezing cold but every night I would walk past the funeral directors knowing my mother was lying in there, cold and on her own and alone. I just did not want her there. I wanted her at home but sadly that wasn't a reality.

I can remember lying on her bed crying. I did not change the pillow. I had to smell her and feel she was still there. I would cuddle her cardigan and wish and pray that my mother would let me know she's ok. I remember falling asleep one particular night and I dreamed my mother was sitting at the top end of the bed where I saw her covered in blood, but in the dream my mother had my father's big overcoat around her shoulders. Suddenly my mother stood up and my father's overcoat would fall and disappear and my mother turned around to look at me and she looked so beautiful. She looked in her 30s, her hair so beautiful, her beautiful blouse; she looked amazing! I held my arms out in the dream as I stood at the bottom of the bed. As she walked towards me I put my arms around my mum and said, "I love you, Mum." She looked up at me and smiled and proceeded to walk out of the door of the bedroom as if she was leaving the flat. She looked so beautiful.

I actually felt that my arms were around my mother as if I was holding her, as if it was real. It felt so real, even in my arms I could feel my mother pressing with her shoulders into my arms. Just felt so real, her face looked so beautiful, she looked so young, she drifted away through the door. My mother gave me the last vision from that bed of her looking beautiful, she didn't want me thinking and seeing what I last saw of her lying there covered in blood. She wanted me to see her smiling and looking beautiful and she truly had done that for me. God bless your beautiful soul, I love you, thank you, for coming to me in my dream, to let me know you were ok, what with dad's big coat around you indicating to me dad came to get you.

On various nights I would be drifting off to sleep. I then suddenly would have an ice-cold wind blowing past my face. It was so cold it would take my breath away. But within my dream state, the arms of my spirit would reach out to my mother as if to cuddle her as I knew in my dream state she was there but my arms actually felt like they were moving to cuddle her like it was electricity of my spirit reaching out for my mother. It was beautiful but the ice-cold wind was so cold past my face, still it was a beautiful feeling of peace. This happened twice in a short space of time. It gave me reassurance that there was something else we all go to, there is another energy, there is something beyond this life on earth that gave me hope and faith and belief that we all would meet again.

The funeral directors asked me if I wished to see my mother in the chapel of rest. I wished. I immediately said, yes. The funeral directors explained to me that my mother had deteriorated, so please expect her not to be as she once was when I knew her. I still had to see her. I had to kiss her goodbye until we met again. I had to be beside her. I had to hold her hand one more time. I entered the funeral directors and a lovely lady by the name of Sharon walked me to the chapel of rest where my mother lay in her coffin. As I walked in the door, my heart and soul were pulled so deeply, so painfully, as I saw the top of my mum's head sticking out of the top of the coffin. The lovely lady closed the door behind me for just a second. I stood back and then proceeded to walk forward towards her. As I did so, the lights in the room, flickered on and off. That was my mother letting me know she was there with me. My mum was extremely spiritual. She believed in the afterlife, she had faith in Jesus, Mother Mary, the almighty God. She had so much faith and with that those lights flickered on and off. It was just my mother letting me know she was there. I had picked up my mother's lipstick from home which she always wore regularly and I decided to make sure she had her lipstick on as she never went out of the front door without her lipstick on. It was a ritual for my mother to look beautiful as she walked out the door. Even if she was putting the bins out she wanted to look glamorous. So, I wanted to make sure she had her lipstick on before she walked through the gates of heaven with my father. I wanted her to look beautiful for my father.

The tears ran down my face. I battled heartache and cried. I held my mum's ice-cold hand and I would not let it go. I stood over my mother and I told her how much I loved her and to say l was so sorry for the son I was as a failure, to have let her down through life. I would never forgive myself for being the son that I was albeit in the years told by my sister how horrible I was, I did end up believing it and with that I said, "So sorry" to my mother. I held her hand even longer as it began to feel warm where I was holding her hand for so long. I kissed my mother's face so many times and cried. My tears fell onto her face. I then proceeded to tell her to call me when it was my time, and to come and get me when it was my time to go from this Earth.

The realisation of this whole situation was still not real. Not reality, it still had not happened, it was as if it was a terrible nightmare and maybe I would wake any minute from this nightmare but there was no awakening. I continued to hold my mother's hand and tell her how much I loved her. I could see her face, it was not her normal self. She was ice-cold, her hair still dyed blonde, and she still was my mother but like at birth the umbilical cord was cut, in death again the umbilical cord of life to my soul and my mother's soul was severed, it was cut. She was now proceeding into the other life and for me to continue on this earth and fight for justice for her. Eventually one of the funeral directors came to get me, and I remembered once again that second feeling as you walk out of a room, a look behind of the physical being of the person that you have lost and as that door closes it's the last second of the visual contact of the one that you love and the door closes. This is very final.

My mother had originally instructed my sister to deal with the funeral arrangements. I ended up dealing with the whole funeral. I had managed to obtain an opera singer, a tenor, to sing Ave Maria by my mother's grave and for two beautiful white doves to be released from my mother's grave into the sky, as two angels, my mother and my father to fly away together into heaven. Two souls, two white beautiful doves to be released. The day of the funeral was excruciating. My sister decided to hold my hand in the car and I struggled with the fact that the feeling of my sister holding my hand was not real. The feeling of love was not real. I believe my sister did feel guilty for the way she treated me during my younger days and even into my adult years. I believe there was an element of guilt there but the damage had been done. There was no return once something was seen. Once something has happened, it's happened. The feeling of holding my sister's hand felt wrong but I wanted to show that I was there for her in her time of need. The funeral was beautiful, the service was amazing but one realisation of how I stood with the family was very obvious.

My ex-girlfriend, Daniella, came to pay her respects to my mother as Daniella loved my mother and equally my mother loved her too. It was extremely kind of her to come and pay respects and one that I truly respect dearly. However, something was very apparent within the church as during the Covid pandemic we were only allowed certain numbers. Still, we had the ample number of 30 people to attend my mother's service. As the normal procedure would be, the family would sit in front of the chapel, by my mother's coffin, which everybody did. As everybody sat down all my sister's family, her daughter, her son and her ex-boyfriend, all sat together on the left-hand side of the chapel. This indicated to me the divide between myself and that side of the family. There was no love, there was no feeling for me at that particular moment in time as I sat on the right-hand side on a bench, completely and solely on my own.

I felt extremely lonely. Not one of them decided to come and sit with me to console me, to make me feel comforted in my hour and moment of need. Nobody would have known if we were not in the same household together, which we had been over a period of weeks, if not months. Nobody sat beside me from that side of the family.

Daniella walked down to the front of the chapel and tapped me on the shoulder and said, "Why are you sitting on your own? Why isn't anybody sitting with you?" She could see I had tears in my eyes as I was crying. I proceeded to tell Daniella, "It's ok darling, I'm fine." This was someone else looking from the outside of a family circle and could see the divide between myself, and my sister and her family. I was an outsider. I had always been an outsider. I was never accepted and my sister proceeded to even turn my daughter against me with her daughter questioning why my daughter placed a post on Facebook regarding her Nan. Yes, my daughter had not seen her Nan for almost several years which was heart-breaking to me as I tried for so many years to forge a bond between my daughter and her Nan but it was to no avail, there was no connection made. I was on my own but I believe that was for a reason and I believe my mother was sitting next to me. That comforted me albeit I couldn't feel or see anybody next to me and I felt extremely alone and isolated, but I wanted to believe my mother was sitting next to me.

The service was beautiful and we proceeded to the funeral itself at our local cemetery. I had a beautiful set of rosary beads that my lovely friend, Grace, had given me. As my mother was being lowered into the ground with my father I placed the rosary beads on top of my mother's coffin. I was still in disbelief that this was happening. I still was not accepting my mother was dead and gone, but the consoling part of all this was that she was now with her husband that she's missed for so many years. As the service came to an end, I stayed and leaned over the hole when my mother was laid and said the Lord's prayer in my mind and tried to get to grips with reality in some strange way.

Many of my beautiful friends came to support including my lovely, dear friend, Clint, and my dear friends, Mark, Paul and Tanya and many more. It was so beautiful to know that I had strength in friends as I was now very alone in a very dark world and no real family that loved me. I set the sights to return home to a lonely flat. We had a small gathering and my dear friends decided to go home. Claire was another dear, ex-girlfriend that came to support me. This was extremely kind of her after the years we were together. We became friends again after explaining my life's journey and the reasons why I was not a very nice person and I admitted my wrongs and how horrible I was. Yet these people knew deep down that wasn't really me.

As the evening approached the reality set in. I set my sights on fighting my mother's case which I proceeded to do over the forthcoming weeks. I was not giving up until I obtained some form of justice. BBC News south east did an amazing story on my mother's case. They were a tremendous support to me in bringing awareness for dispensary errors and that the potential effects of a dispensary error could end up as a cause of death.

What I needed to do was create as much awareness as I could. This was my goal and I proceeded to do so over the weeks and months ahead. The next uncertainty was the flat which I was in. It was a housing society accommodation which my mother had lived in originally with my father in 1992. As stated I was my mother's primary carer for over a year as a registered carer and with that I proceeded to apply for my residency of the flat with a hope that I got it, as not only would I have to contend with my mother's death I would have to contend with being homeless.

But this was not the end of heartache. Lyrah's funeral date was also set which was the 17th of February 2021. I knew this would be another heart-breaking day as I proceeded to attend the crematorium and watched the limo arrive with a little white coffin with Lyrah's body within. I still could not comprehend, as only a week or so previously I was there with my mother, seeing my mother being laid to rest and now I was seeing a little nine-year old also being laid to rest.

I loved little Lyrah. I will never forget her. She will always be locked in my heart until the moment I close my eyes and meet her again. She will never leave my heart.

I truly felt for her mother. Victoria, Lorna, and the family and the children had to see their beautiful sister laid to rest and for a mother to see her child leave this world is beyond any words incomprehensible in any way. No words fitted the feeling of that particular moment in time. The service was beautiful, so many beautiful words were said for a very beautiful, little girl. I battled the tears within me, but for the moment little Lyrah was alive within my mind with happy memories, which for those moments in time, everybody forgot the journey ahead and just enjoyed the moment. That for me gave me a smile in my heart, that I had created those smiles.

The experience of life in front of me was one I just could not understand. The past experience of my life, I still did not understand, but knew the damage that life had done to me. Everybody in life has a story to tell everybody lives with experiences that either makes them or breaks them. We lose loved ones that we love and care for, sometimes. If a loved one passes peacefully it's acceptable to a degree, albeit heart-breaking, but you can learn to accept that loss. But accepting a loss in a tragic way with circumstances that are not of the normal nature like watching my mother choking on her own blood, fighting for her life, is difficult. Fighting for her life was not the image I would have imagined for my mother to leave this world and for Lyrah's family to realise one day their daughter was going to leave this world due to an inoperable brain tumour is something most certainly no mother should live to experience. No father, no relative of that child, should experience that loss so soon, so tragically.

There came a point where I wanted to say 'goodbye' to my sister. I did this by way of a text message. I could not deal with it over the phone or in person. I did not want to see her, I did not want any contact with her. The damage she had done between myself and my daughter was the end result by her, and her daughter having words by message to my daughter which upset her. My daughter never attended my mother's funeral, her Nan's, because of this, which further broke my heart and made me feel extremely lonely and alone. It broke my heart beyond words. I tried for so many years from her age of 11 years up until 20 years, I took her to see her Nan every weekend and yet she did not find the need to attend or support me, her father, in any way. That was devastating to me as we had never ever had any disagreement in life.

My last message from my daughter was, "Sorry I could not attend today but wish you well." A lot of this was down to my sister and her daughter's poisoning. Some weeks later after that message, my

175

daughter decided to disown me and completely took me off of her social media which I never realised had happened, but that further broke my heart as now I had no family around me at all in the darkest moments of my life. I have never felt so alone in my entire life. I was a broken man and further thoughts of suicide arose in my mind. Further thoughts of ending my life became strong again, as everything I've ever loved has hurt me and broken me. For some reason everyone it felt, was out to destroy me and this was stemming, all, from one person that created all this damage, which was my sister, so with this in mind I decided it was time to say goodbye.

I sent a lengthy text message to my sister explaining my feelings. I did not want to see her or meet her or talk to her on the phone. It was time to end our relationship as brother and sister after the damage that was done to me as a child, suffering with many forms of emotional child abuse from her and the evil words that she used to say to me which had never left me. I was always made out to be the bad, horrible, nasty little boy and eventually not only did my sister turn my daughter against me she also turned my mother against me. I was always the outsider of the whole family. My sister poisoned everybody's mind to turn against me. It all sounds paranoid but this was reality. I was always bullied and intimidated and made to feel worthless, small and unimportant in life. This turned me into that person I was programmed as a child from the age of seven years old. I recalled many horrible moments from being locked in the bedroom and sexually assaulted by her friend which was instigated by my sister. The feelings were all pure evil and into my later life in the moments of being told she never loved me as a brother. It was time to say goodbye and I did so and put all my feelings down in the text message and sent it.

Within a few hours I received a message from her daughter telling me I was nothing but a joke. This only confirmed to me the feelings of that side of the family, the sitting in the chapel on my own at my mother's funeral service, everything fuelled one outcome - I had the choice now to not be bullied anymore or made to feel worthless. I had the choice to turn my back on the negativity that was portrayed to me from a very young age. I was going to close the door on that feeling for the rest of my eternal life. Whatever days that I had left, it was time for me to close that door and seal that door shut. My mother explained to my sister prior to her death some weeks or maybe months or years before about all her little items of precious goods which were of no value but were sentimental to my mother. My mother left all her jewellery to my sister's daughter. My mother also proceeded to leave all her religious items to my sister's ex-boyfriend and all her crystal cut glass which had been handed down through her sister when she passed away - all that was left to my sister and other items of sentimental value were left to my sister's son. At no point did my mother think of me. Not one item of sentimental value to say 'thank you son for being in my life'. I had realised my sister had turned my mother against me for decades. This pretty much was from the moment of my birth. I only learnt to understand that from issues of being locked in bedrooms, being bullied and intimidated, it only became apparent to me how much my sister hated me. I loved her so much, I always only wanted to be loved but failed to understand the meaning of that magical word called love. I had lost all reality with learning how to love when I looked over my relationships. Every one of them was a failure as I didn't believe they loved me because always when I loved people I believed I was being betrayed behind my back. I learnt to live that way from childhood which I then portrayed into my adult years and failed to believe anyone within any relationship that they actually loved me. When they told me 'I love you', I didn't believe them. This was a trait that was instilled in me from my childhood and carried into my adult life.

I said goodbye to my sister and I received no reply. This only indicated that she admitted to herself what she had done to me. There was no defence put up, there was no reply, there was no nothing, this was admittance, and for me it was farewell and in its strange way I wished her well. I wished her no harm. I wrote in the message, 'I truly wish you the very best in life but we as a family, as a brother and sister we are done'. I sadly had no further contact with my daughter. She decided to close the door on me due to the results of how my sister and her daughter had treated her which had no doing from me. To walk away so easily broke my heart.

The inquest date was set for my mother. I had battled for many months for many hours in front of a laptop. My heart was broken and lonely. I had never felt so isolated and lonely in all my life as all the people that I thought loved me, all they did was hurt me. I continued to fight everyday with the purpose of obtaining some kind of justice for my mother. My sister had no interest as such to the outcome and never asked previously. I have never been the type of person to give up on a fight especially if I believed in the journey ahead, to fight for what I truly believed in, I would never walk away. During the inquest which was the second part of two inquests, I had to deal with the head consultant on my mother's ward during the night of her admittance to Medway Hospital. I then had to deal with the pathologist that carried out the post-mortem on my mother the head of the pharmacy and a separate doctor employed by the pharmacy. This was all done by video link during the inquest. My dear Ann, who sat beside me throughout the inquest, was a great support for me.

During the inquest I had taken notes and remembered the pathologist explaining to me during the post mortem that he had found no signs of Covid-19 on my mother's lungs, there was no pneumonia, there were no signs of any Covid on my mother's lungs. I proceeded to ask: how could my mother receive a positive Covid-19 test result when there was no Covid present on my mother's lungs? The pathologist gave me no real answer to my question, other than that the consultant had examined my mother specifically and said the reason why my mother had gastrointestinal haemorrhage was due to the (Mallory Weiss tear) by repeated coughing which can cause haemorrhage. Yes, my mother had a cough but she had had a cough for a period of years, a very light, annoying, as if tickly, cough. She was a smoker and she had COPD chronic obstructive pulmonary disorder and had Ventolin pumps and medication to keep that under control. I proceeded to ask the pathologist again as it appeared that the coroner wanted to put my mother's death down, as 'primary cause Covid-19'.

I struggled with the fact that no Covid was found on my mother's lungs so how could my mother's primary cause of death be noted as Covid-19? And secondary cause of death gastrointestinal haemorrhage? I failed to understand how my mother's death could be put down as Covid 19 when there was no Covid present on my mother's lungs. Further to the pathologist's examination all that was found on my mother's lungs was slight water which was a result of my mother's heart not working correctly.

I discovered one thing in life, that in the majority of professions whether that be Medical, Government or Police, whatever the profession, they all stick together. My mother did not have Covid-19 as no Covid-19 was on her lungs at all or pneumonia. One thing was certain that the whole of the medical profession that day covered up the fact of what truly happened to my mother. Covid-19 was the perfect excuse to not show the outcome as medical negligence in which the pharmacist gave my mother Fluoxetine which caused my mother gastrointestinal haemorrhage, as it is one of the side effects of this drug on its own, let alone being mixed with Clopidogrel which would further cause gastrointestinal haemorrhage, bleeding of the oesophagus and stomach.

I had done a fair amount of research into the drugs in question and I knew if it was not for the fact of my mother's death being put down as Covid-19, I had a strong case against the pharmacy for negligence. It had felt like my mother had been murdered and I failed to be able to obtain justice for my mother. BBC News south east was there to also do further news coverage on my mother's case. My mother's death was put down to Covid-19 as a primary cause of death. I knew in my heart of hearts this was a medical cover up. I had no legal representation other than myself in a coroner's court with a multi-million-pound pharmaceutical company that had lawyers on serious amounts of money to take me on.

We live in a world of massive corruption on every level. It is apparent in day to day life, it's not what you do, it's who you know. Cover-ups are on every level in life. The government, in my opinion, are the biggest legal gangsters walking on the face of the planet and that goes for every government in any world. They all work to their own rules. It's just the way life is. The police at the high end of the police force are exceptionally corrupt. I knew as regards even my case what a police informant had done to me, to manufacture a crime, to incite me into a manufactured crime that had no intention to be carried out, as it was police officers that were the armed robbers pointing fingers at me for shooting people in which I had no involvement. A ridiculous amount of tax-payers' money spent on nothing that came to nothing other than housing me, giving me three meals a day in prison, which cost thousands and thousands of pounds - for what? For nothing which actually happened.

The same went for this inquest. Most likely the pathologist's husband plays golf with a consultant who most likely has dinner at the medical functions with the pharmacist that gave my mother the incorrect medication and a doctor most likely is having an affair with the pathologist's wife - it's just the way that it is. Whatever level of profession, there is corruption and within your profession it's nature you will all look out for each other's backs and that's what happened at my mother's inquest. That very day I returned home and was further broken so where do I go from here? As what's now my new path of this new chapter of the journey of the rest of my life? If so, what do I do now to reinvent myself? I've already done it once by changing my name from Clive Sands to Rocky Amore so what do I do? Change my name again to be another person? The answer is 'no'.

I now have no family present in my life. Those that loved me have disowned me and those that were family that portrayed they loved me have betrayed me. I had lived a life of a lie for so many years. From a child into adult life I lived a lie, behind my mask of me! I pretended to be somebody else to escape who I really, truly was and that was a beaten child emotionally scarred from the bullying and intimidation and child abuse on every level.

I now enter a new chapter in my life, to the reinvention of this new world I am entering which is lonely and cold. I then have to find me, who I really am, finding me after 52 years of life on this earth, being lied to by my entire family even my own mother whom I loved with all my heart, who towards the end of her life due to my sister poisoning her mind for decades left me out from a little gift to give out to the family as a sentiment of love. Once she had passed it was her verbal words which she left with my sister which speaks volumes, because how do I know if she actually did leave me something to remember her by? I didn't want money, we never had that privilege. Ever we were broke. I would have loved an item of thought, of love. Due to the way my sister was with me I'm never going to know even if I was left a wedding ring or an eternity ring that my father gave her. It would have been a momentous, beautiful, sentimental gift I would have carried for the rest of my life but there was nothing and I was going on the word of my sister so I live in a world of uncertainty of a family that had no stability of those magical words of truth and love.

So, I will pass you my judgement on my experience of what we call life. I have shared with you my journey of this life with the hope that someone could relate to my experience and with this in mind maybe take away something from this. I will give you the outcome of this story and the moral of this story in my final word. My final word comes from my heart as everything I have written within this book is of the pure truth and nothing but the truth. I wanted to tell the world about my life. Some people may want to read about it, some people may want to laugh at it, however it was my story to tell. It's been my journey to a destination, as they say, it's the final place of discovery and I will pass you now my final word.

The Final Word

Here within this book I have given you my life's experiences. I have shared my feelings, my emotions and my journey. I have stayed silent for many years. I have not spoken about my life openly before but I felt the need to do so. Learning to open up about your feelings is an essential guide to healing a damaged soul and deal with mental health issues. I have reached the crossroads of life. A new chapter. Everybody has a story to tell, everybody has a journey; some are more shortened than others and some are lengthy journeys with a world of experience within them. I believe we can learn from other people's experiences in life. If one can take a small part of someone else's experience and learn from it, maybe it could be a blessing in disguise.

My entire life has been a lie. I have hidden behind my mask long enough. It is now time to remove the mask and reveal the true me. As you would have read throughout this book, throughout my childhood I had a strong negative influence and that was an elder sister, almost ten years my senior. That negative influence programmed a very young mind to believe it was of a nasty nature. Over time an innocent child lives to believe they are that person. This will reflect in your child's temperament whilst growing up which also can affect later in life as an adult. We all have the responsibility to show children the right paths.

This negative influence can come from a brother, sister, mother or father or even from school at an early age. What a young set of eyes witnesses whilst growing up is the programming of a young mind that knows no better other than what it sees and listens to. It's very easy to say a child knows right from wrong. This is right to a degree but it's the lessons we show to them which determines the outcome. A child would go to school to learn about life. We, as adults, live a life of schooling and of learning. At the age of fifty-two I have learnt so much more about life and am still learning. The learning process never ends.

It is essential as a parent to be aware of these negative influences - for example, bullying, intimidation and all levels of child abuse from sexual to emotional abuse, keeping a strong awareness of these negative influences which is an essential guide for a child's journey into later years of life. I endured negative influences from a sister ten years my senior which made my life completely hell from the age of seven years; which made me believe I was a horrible, little boy which programmed me to become horrible. I can categorically say to you, this almost took my life. I ended up in prison. I became violent, aggressive. I took drugs and drank excessive amounts of alcohol.

My life was made hell for many years and into my adult life. The person that did this to me also had a negative influence in her life. As a child my sister witnessed her father as a violent, aggressive alcoholic from a very young age. This programmed my sister to become that person who was an aggressive, violent, drug taking alcoholic. The domino effect this has throughout life within a family can have devastating effects later in life. Some people can skip this and be blessed with a fortunate journey and get away from the negative influence at an early age, but in many cases, this can result in a heart-breaking journey.

The next question is: can I forgive the negative influence that tormented my soul for many years? The answer to that question is: yes. The reason being, the person truly to blame from the outset is her violent alcoholic father. One thing I cannot forget.

As an adult any one of us can walk away from any negativity that is pulling you into a dark place but a child can't escape this. In adult life we recognise the damage that's been done to us and we learn that we have a choice. I could never forget the damage that had been done to me. The emotional abuse that I received as a child reflected in my later life and it's only now, at fifty- two years of age, I can close the door and leave those feelings locked away. They will never go away and they will still affect my life every day but we learn to deal with our emotions.

To contemplate suicide shows a heart and soul that is at the end of its road. That is a tremendously dark place that nobody should ever consider walking into. Twice I have contemplated suicide, the second attempt put me in hospital. This was a wake-up call to life as when it finally came to close my eyes on this life I didn't want to go. My mother and my father gave me the most beautiful gift that I could ever receive in life, and that is life.

During the 70s, 80s and even during the 90s mental health was not in the forefront of concern. Specifically, for men we were told to "man up". For a man to even cry, you would appear weak. I have lost very close friends that have suffered serious mental health issues due to their past reflecting on their later life which has resulted in suicide. Mental health issues in children is very much high these days with children contemplating suicide and some actually taking their life. Truly tragic.

I urge all you people to learn how to talk, open up your feelings either to a friend or seek professional counselling. I had battled mental health issues from childhood, it's only now I finally am dealing with those demons.

The experiences I've shared with you in this book are all true, and in many cases, there are people that have suffered far worse journeys and some that have suffered very little, and some never survived to tell their tale. Everyone walks the journey of life, not everyone learns to understand its meaning and some sadly never get to deal with mental health.

The meaning of life. For me the meaning of life is to smile. We all hide behind a smile. Sometimes it covers up a multitude of emotional pain but taking the time to make another person smile costs you nothing, the infectious feeling it brings is amazing. The most important value of life is realising everything is temporary, nothing lasts forever. Your life is not permanent on this earth and the most tragic thing I have experienced is that at any age your life can be taken. Material things can always be replaced. You could lose everything. However, you have the chance to replace everything. The most valuable gift that you have is your life. You have one chance to live it. There is no rehearsal and there is no second chance to realise how fragile our existence truly is.

I have lost everything in my life that I have loved. Love has betrayed me in every aspect of the word. I failed to understand its beauty when all the people that I have loved have hurt me in some form or another. My beautiful father I lost at a very early age. I loved him so dearly, he showed me love in his own way. I never had the chance to embrace my father with love or even tell him I love him. My mother also was not of an affectionate nature. Very little love was shown and when she left this world she gave her heart to everybody else except the one person that lived and loved by her side, albeit yes, I took the wrong journey at times, which I live with many regrets in doing so, but I loved my mother. She was poisoned by a negative influence which destroyed her love for me over decades, which I realised more after my mother's passing.

Regarding my sister's jealousy of my relationship with my mother and my father, which my sister never had from her father which I am so sorry for, my mother adored my sister. Her father from my mother's first marriage was an aggressive, violent alcoholic which rubbed off on my sister, which affected her life and my relationship with my mother. My negative sister turned my daughter against me over my mother's death. She set out to ruin my life in so many ways. The one beautiful gift that I had left in my life was my daughter which was destroyed by a very negative influential sister and her daughter - the love I had for my daughter, which I showed and made sure she knew I loved her, from her age of eleven years when I came out of prison. I maintained a level of reliability and a strong level of love. Sadly, my daughter decided to walk away from my life for which I cannot blame her as the negativity that was given to her from my sister and her daughter over my mother's death was unforgivable. I lost another part of my soul.

Another aspect of life I have learnt is that you cannot make somebody love you if it isn't in their heart, it just isn't possible. I have learnt to walk away from people that don't share your path. Do not waste your time on people that don't respect your journey. I have learnt that loyalty is a word used extremely loosely in today's world. Loyalty today has no real meaning and this goes from blood related family to friends. If someone cannot reciprocate loyalty to you then do not waste your time and effort as we are only here for a very short space of time. Do not waste those precious seconds, minutes and hours on people that have no use in your journey other than drain your energy in walking your path.

My perception of this world today is that there is corruption on every level of life. The Government are the biggest legal gangsters walking on the face of this earth. The corruption within Parliament which has clearly been proved throughout the years of the secret handshakes, the Freemason meetings, the brown envelopes passing hands, and the rules and regulations broken to suit their own needs and the regulations twisted to fit their needs.

The police specifically during the 70s, 80s and more so the 90s were incredibly corrupt as my own personal experience within this book reveals, to obtain statistics showing levels of crime dropping. The police would go to many underhand paths to get crime levels down. Within the high level of the walls of New Scotland Yard, within their very secret little unit that they have, drugs would be planted, firearms would be planted, manufactured crimes to incite criminals into crime. In English law during those years, entrapment was no defence. If the police wanted you off the streets they would do so. This is just life being life, it's how life works.

I was sentenced to seven years for conspiracy to rob a nightclub in which two undercover police officers were the armed robbers who even acted out with permission of the nightclub. The robbery, to look like a robbery was taking place, but of course in a half discreet manner just in case I was watching, to make sure they did the job. This was all instigated by a registered police informant that was working closely with the police for many years.

Entrapment Is no defence in English law but is considered to be an abuse of the process of the court for agents to lure a person into committing illegal acts and then to seek to prosecute him for doing so. I learned to take my punishment as even though it was a police sting, I would have taken the money if it was a real robbery so I deserved what I got; just not the way it was done so underhand. There is corruption within the Medical Profession. Cover-ups which I have experienced first-hand and the elderly being given too much morphine to move them on out of this life. Cases of the elderly being neglected, disregarded, after all they have contributed to this life; they are disregarded when they become elderly. They have no use financially to this society. How tragic that really is, that you only have a certain amount of time that you are of use to this world and when you become elderly you become forgotten. I experienced this with my dear mother due to a pharmacy error which I know took my mother's life which was all covered up with COVID 19 as my mother's primary cause of death. I watched my mother choke to death on her own blood. A vision that will never leave me.

On every level of occupation there is corruption. The brown envelope of cash into the back pocket of your local MP along with your local councillor too, even the local contractor for the work you wish to obtain. Money talks. Don't kid yourself otherwise. So, my word to you within the criminal world or even those that are looking to enter it, take this advice and take it very close to your hearts - there is no loyalty in the criminal world, none whatsoever. If you think there is a moral code of conduct forget it. It's extremely rare. The criminal world of today is kids stabbing one another, teenagers shooting one another for a reputation. We, the world, are responsible for all this. This can be changed by showing how gaining a reputation of true respect comes from helping others in life. What has this world come to which has programmed children, the youth of today, into taking steps to think this is how they should be leading their lives in such a manner? It's tragic, truly tragic. If this story could put off one teenager from committing crime then that is a blessing. There is no loyalty in crime. And as regards to that world called 'the criminal underworld' it's the biggest load of a pretentious false image of plastic gangsters you would ever find. The real villains are the Government, that is the real underworld! The rising increase in fuel bills by which the legal Gangsters of Government let the poor, elderly sit in the cold as they can't pay their bills whilst members of our Government drive around in their new Range Rovers. Who is the villain? Robbing from the poor and giving to the rich. Humans get greedy. From MPs to the streets, it's a greedy world. Kids killing each other for respect, try telling that to the mothers and fathers, heart-breaking. The way to gain a majority of respect is gained from true paths of people going out there, making a difference in other people's lives by helping the elderly lady across the road with her shopping even buying her shopping for her, not stealing it. Taking the time for someone, for a sick child, a wish come true, what better way to gain respect? So please take note, change your path, reinvent your journey and live with a smile without having to look over your shoulder.

We live in a very aggressive world. Everybody is going 100 mph to get somewhere fast disregarding the person in front of you or even looking back at the person behind you. People have no time for people anymore. Gone are the days of your neighbour knocking on your door to check if you're ok. Everybody is too afraid to step outside their front door in case they get stabbed or robbed. What a horrible world to live in, living in fear! Take a moment and step back and look at life and its reason for you to be here. We all have a purpose here on this earth to live constructively and happily. It is the art of life to do what makes you happy. It is the most essential gift you could give yourself.

This world in my opinion has already been destroyed. We, over the decades, have killed this planet. We have countries with excessive heat to the point of melting car bumpers and headlights. Even within the UK we have reached temperatures of over 40 degrees which is unheard of in the UK. The ozone layer has taken its battering for far too long. All the electric cars in the world are not going to prevent the damage that has been done to this beautiful world which we have all destroyed and contributed to destruction, to a degree.

Within the next fifty years you will see drastic changes to this planet. I thankfully will not be alive to witness it but I feel sorry for those growing up, the children of those years. I fear for their welfare in their journey into this world. It's so very sad that this beautiful planet has been destroyed by humankind. We are meant to be a world of intelligence but with all levels of intelligence there is ignorance, the results of which we are witnessing now. You hear of tsunamis, you hear of water levels diminishing, you hear of wildlife dying and being wiped out in certain areas of the world, certain species becoming extinct. I worry for this world that we live in. My experiences within this book are so minimal compared to the outcome of many that have lived. My shared experiences have shown me it's the influence of others that can determine someone else's journey and this is my experience in a minimal form. Lead by example, and if world leaders can destroy this world what chance do we have?

I would like to think that we could extend the longevity of this beautiful planet by taking the time to love one another in a way that shows we care for one another. Love is the most magical emotion of life. To live a life not experiencing that magical gift called love, is tragic. Love comes in many forms. Learn to live with that in your heart. I almost destroyed myself from not experiencing the magic of love. I am only now learning to embrace it as we, as a world, have become a selfish planet. Not taking the time to share such a positive energy is so sad.

We have the option, we have the choice to not let the past haunt us. It will never leave us but the art of this journey of what we call life is that we have to sometimes reinvent our journey, reinvent us as a person, and start a new chapter. Turn the page to a clean slate and rewrite your future. We all have the option to do that and make everything around us a better place which will result in your children being brought into a happier world, a happier environment. Social media has destroyed many children's lives. To live up to the expectations of what children see on social media, the social acceptance of how many likes you would receive, how can your life be better than the other child or person and this goes for adults too. With the continuation of the requirement of self-acceptance, showing a life that is not real, the majority of people that continuously post images of a happy place of selfies, self-gratification and the need to feel social media famous. I fail to understand all of this. Today's world lives off a phone. You have people walking in front of you with their head scrolling up and down, with their eyes transfixed on their phone. People take their phones to the toilet and into the bathroom. Their life revolves around a phone. The art of connection between two humans is sadly becoming a rarity.

We as a nation have discovered that social media can also result in serious mental health issues, from young children through teenagers into adults, even leading to suicides. This is the requirement of social media acceptance, the tragic outcome of today's world we live in. Children and teenagers will sit in front of their TV on the Xbox playing violent games which increases aggressive mental activity and once again the programming of a young mind computing its journey. Now we are seeing the outcome of this on our streets of today with the gang culture that we have.

I wanted to use my experiences albeit very minimal, but I have lived to tell the tale and that for me as I approach my mid-fifties I have learnt a very valuable lesson and that is, we can start again.

I have finally found my purpose on this earth in my little corner of the world where I live. I produce positivity within my community to share an energy that inspires others to create a better place, that gives hope in the darkest times. In recent months I lost a very close friend whose name was Jan. As Jan was closing her eyes on this life after battling cancer she said to me, "I wish I could turn the clock back." In other words, Jan wished she had fulfilled her dreams and taken the time to live her journey the way she imagined happily in her mind. But it was too late. One day we are all going to be gone so why not live your life happily and fulfil every opportunity that life can give you. Make it happen. Money isn't the route to happiness. Your wealth is within your heart; this produces positivity and radiates that magical gift called 'a smile'.

I run a charitable organisation that was named after a beautiful lady called Rebecca that continues to smile. Her life was cut so short due to cancer yet she still smiled and showed strength. That smile has not been forgotten by us all which proves the fact that seeing those muscles move in your face that creates a happy image is an image that can stay with you for eternal life like Rebecca's smile with me. My little charitable organisation called BEKS - Bring Every Kind Smile is my life. It's my entirety along with my little cat called Poppy, the love of my life. We all need a purpose. When we open our eyes in the morning we need to create a positive day. Do not waste your time in a job that has no meaning other than simply paying your bills. If you are not happy with what you're doing every day then you have a choice, do what you love, take the chance to try another avenue. We have one life: do not spend fifty years in a place you're not comfortable with, because once those fifty years are over you cannot go back in time. Like my beautiful friend, Jan, wanted to do, you can't turn the clock back. The seconds and minutes roll forwards not backwards, there is no rewind, there is no second chance.

So, the moral of this whole journey that I have shared with you within this book is that I was starved of love all my life. I failed to understand that magical word called love when all love had ever done was hurt me and destroy me, as everything I loved wanted to kill me, which it nearly did. Surround yourself with real, true people. I have learnt in life, whether it be family or friends, their negativity can destroy your journey. If these people are destroying your journey, close the door on them, find peace, find real people in your life as that can contribute to a happier, real, genuine, honest journey - your people around you are your destiny. Programme the young minds, the children, with love and positivity and honesty, and to be kind to others.

I am very blessed to the beautiful people that have stuck beside me throughout my traumatic time. I have had Keith Blackman and Matt Gibbons of K&M electrical who have become my company sponsors for my charitable organisation. These guys albeit very much younger than me are blessed with a solid family unit of love. My experiences, I share with them, with a view to guide a little positive energy, which I tell them, to grab life now and make it work now. We all will suffer grief sometime in our life, we will grieve the loss of a loved one. After the tragic way my mother died it took my soul with her and the images will never leave me. Along with dealing with PTSD daily I learn to try and do something that makes me smile. We will all have moments of sadness but the people around you, the true people will hold you up and be there until you can stand on your own two feet.

These people will bless your tomorrows and I thank these people that have been kind to me. I apologise deeply to all the people I lost my temper with in the past and present; that was not the real me and was not justified. My dear friend, Clint, who has been my rock, my brother from another mother. His loyalty is impeccable and I love and respect everything about him. I will never forget the support he has given me through the loss of my mother. I would like to mention Mark McAllister who has been a tremendous support for BEKS and as a true friend to me. His wealth of knowledge in running a business has been a wealth of support.

I felt I had lost all my reasons for having a purpose for this life. All my family have gone and those that are left have no time for me to love. I have closed the door on many people and moved on with my life. Some people do not share the same journey and it is pointless trying to obtain crossroads into each other's journey when we have totally different directions. Life is far too short, far too fragile, to waste time in trying.

I will close with my final word and I hope someone can take something from this experience. I didn't want to call this an autobiography because I haven't finished my journey yet. An autobiography takes you to a destination. I haven't reached that destination yet but I am going to get there, and I am going to continue to give something which I was never shown, to all I meet - that love and kindness. This is the reason why I do what I do every day as feeling alone and isolated is a feeling I know only too well, and I do not wish anyone to feel that loneliness without hope. I love helping sick and terminally ill children with a wish or a dream come true right the way up to the elderly to make them feel loved, just to sit and talk to them, let them tell you their stories, share a cup of tea, and give them my time.

And for me to give something that I failed to understand for many years to realise its quality and its purpose, and how essential it is to give someone something so magical, and that is love. When I close my eyes on this life I want to know that I have fulfilled my journey with helping others to feel loved in every aspect of the word, to feel loved, create memories for families that are going to lose a loved one to cancer, a terminal illness, give some kindness, moments in time of happiness which can be created. I have lived a very negative life, I have lived a lie for over fifty years. This was my life's story, a negative lie, a mismatch of misunderstandings of what loyalty was and what love was, so with this I've taken my negative journey and have turned my experiences around and made use of what I failed to understand during my life. Having a purpose, and my purpose is to make you smile. I will tell you how beautiful your hair looks today. I will put my arms around you and tell you how special you are, to tell you I love, whether that be a friend or a loved one, love comes in many different forms. We all as a nation can change the outcome of tomorrow if we just took the time to love one another.

I have experienced many emotions and was told for years I was a horrible person which made me that person. Discovering me again was not easy, but whatever time I have left on this earth, I will learn to love again and give love unconditionally. Being made to feel worthless by anyone in life can destroy you. Thankfully due to the wonderful people that have coached me into a better place, I can live again. I'm far from healed, I will never be but at least I can learn to walk new paths again thanks to kindness from real people that care without motive. Dealing daily with depression is a lifelong battle I will have to endure, but again learn to bless your path with new people as your wisdom will keep the bad people at bay. We live and learn. This book is my opinion on real life.

I have managed to get myself back into my charitable path and am now helping to support a young mother's fight for her little baby boy called Leo for his overseas treatment to save his life, with a view to bring hope and faith and belief back into lost hearts.

Learn to take time for one another, take a moment for nature, embrace its beauty. It's not just for us oldies to start at the root of youth and make that path ahead, one of positivity. Programme young minds to live positively without any negative influences. That's what this story is all about and I hope and I pray it can inspire someone to turn their life around. I'm not finished yet with my journey, I have only just started. I haven't reached my destination. I still have a long way to go to heal my own heart but I promise you that every day I will do something good for someone, something positive. Live with faith and belief. Learn to love yourself and to live your life in peace and live to love your life, and learn to laugh at life too. God bless each and every one of you to a brighter tomorrow. Never give up on what you believe in and find your purpose in life. If you are not happy with your life, learn to reinvent yourself, open a new page of a new chapter of your life and start again. Live through a child's eyes and to live to "Bring Every Kind Smile."

Acknowledgments

Clinton Beadle

You are a brother from another mother. Thank you from the depths of my heart for being a truly amazing friend to me and standing beside me when I lost my mother and for being honest, true and loyal. You have restored my faith in humankind. A truly, selfless man that cares with heart. Thank you. I love you dearly. A true heart.

Sue Beadle

My darling friend, thank you for feeding me, looking after me when I was at my lowest. You're one of life's true angels. You have been a real friend to me and have not left my side throughout my grieving. God bless your soul and thank you for everything. I love you.

Anthony Manning and Tracey Bosman

Thank you both dearly for loving me with sincere hearts. You have shown me love of which I had lost understanding its beauty. You both have been my rocks of support and your help in holding me up when I was falling will never be forgotten. We are family and I truly love you both sincerely. You wiped my tears and saved my soul. Love you both always.

Mark McAllister

You have shown me kindness and belief on new levels for which I will be eternally so thankful. You believed in me when others walked away. Thank you for your guidance and faith in BEKS, my charitable organisation. I will keep bringing those smiles, thanks to your support.

And truly thank you for the assistance, for getting this book ready. Sincerely, so appreciated.

Keith Blackman and Matt Gibbons

I will be eternally grateful for your kindness and faith in BEKS, for your sponsoring my charitable organisation. Your passion to succeed as K&M Electrical has shown how you both keep your word on all you do and that goes for BEKS. So appreciated.

Daniel Colquit and Jayna Colquit

Thank you for being so kind when I was in a very bad way, when I lost my mother. You brought food round to me and made sure I had eaten. Thank you for caring with such kind hearts.

Joy Zarine

My dear friend, Joy. Thank you for you amazing guidance with publishing my book. Your knowledge was a blessing. And if this is fortunate to become a film, that red carpet awaits you. God bless and thank you.

Arthur Ellis (Medway Community Mental Health Team)

Dear Arthur, your understanding of my pain was a blessing and showing my faith was my strength to the next chapter of my life. God bless you and thank you genuinely for all your sincerity and guidance.

Paul Fryer

My dear loyal, true friend. Thank you for being a true strength of support. Even though you were going through a heart-breaking journey with your dear father battling dementia, you still found the time to call me and check on me. You have been a true, loyal friend to me which I will never ever forget. I love you with all my heart.

Andy Clarke

Since our release from Her Majesty's big house we have remained friends throughout for which I sincerely thank you. For all those crazy memories made which I will never forget. Thank you for the smiles made, they will stay within my heart forever.

Tracy Jane Hodges

You are our Pinky, always will be. Thank you for being my dear friend since my release from prison. I will never forget all those crazy mad nights, clubbing. Thank you for the lovely memories made.

Emma Trickery (Woodlands Family Practice)

Thank you for your amazing support throughout with my mental health. As doctors, all of you at the practice have gone above and beyond to help me. Eternally grateful.

Mark Farrelly

You gave me your time when you battled mental health daily. You picked me up and took me for a drive and talked to me with understanding. I will never forget your true, caring kindness. Thank you so much my dear friend.

Paul Knight and Tanya Knight

My very dear friends, you both have walked on my journey for many years. You loved me with true hearts, wiped my tears, supported my life throughout and have been there when I had fallen. I will be eternally thankful for showing me the truth when my walls had fallen in. God bless you both. I love you both always.

Richard Sandman

My dear true friend, thank you for taking the time to show me true friendship and standing beside BEKS with projects and giving me loyal support from R Sandman builders. You have been a rock of loyalty. I can't thank you enough. You're a true friend.

Robby Crozier and Carmel Crozier

My two true friends that have not left my side. You both have shown me in my darkest times that friends can be truly stronger than family and for that your friendship has been a blessing of love. Thank you both for caring.

Jamie Ali

My dear friend, thank you for all your kindness when I lost my dear mother. Your messages and calls gave me smiles of hope and your understanding of mental health was a true building block of strength. God bless you.

Wendy Mills and Ian Mills

My dear friends your warmth and sincerity has been a blessing. In the months of isolation after losing my dear mother you helped me back into society by inviting me to your lovely wedding which helped me regain strength again. Your loyalty is true and real. I love and respect you both with true sincerity. Your understanding and support will never be forgotten. God bless you both.

Sean Kennedy

God bless you. You came through from the darkness to show me faith and took the time to take me to your safe place and that has been my saviour. The Lord has shown me that light, and your guidance has been a true blessing. Thank you sincerely. God bless you.

Jay Usher

We have maintained friendship since we were released from Her Majesty's big house and many happy memories have been made which I will never forget. Thank you for standing beside me at my mother's graveside. With all my heart, thank you for your kind sincere support.

Andy Gower

I can't thank you enough for taking the time to sit with me at my mother and father's grave when I was at my lowest point. I will never forget your truly kind friendship to me. Thank you for being there for me.

Ann and John

Thank you, Ann, for supporting me during my mother's inquest. It is so truly appreciated. You and John have been real support and it will never be forgotten. God bless you and all your lovely family.

Julie Lucus and Mark Lucus

Your guidance in our counselling sessions have been true and pure, helping me open the doors to a beaten heart and soul that failed to believe that light was possible. You and Mark have been true and it will never be forgotten, all your selfless time in helping me walk again into the light. God bless you both.

Matt Cross

You have been a lifelong, true friend and your support to me when I lost my mother was beyond words a true support to me. It will never be forgotten my friend. Even though you were battling with your health you still gave me your time. Thank you sincerely. Love you.

Brian Long

You have been my true rock of loyal support since the day we walked out of those prison gates. We shared many crazy moments that will never leave me. We certainly caused an eruption but ones that made us laugh and smile. Thank you, my lovely, loyal friend. God bless you. Love you.

Joe Egan

Mike Tyson named you, 'The toughest white man on the planet'. I could write a thousand sentences on your kind, loyal, true heart. You have been a true support to my charitable organisation (BEKS) for many years, and a true friend to me too. I name you, 'The kindest white man on the planet.' Thank you, Joe, for your friendship and support for me as a friend, and my charity. I love you. God bless.

Matt Legg

My dear friend not only have you stood in the ring with the best, you gave me a shot at being your friend, which I sincerely love and respect. Your true friendship has been a strength to me and an amazing support to my charitable organisation (BEKS). I love you. God Bless.

Dene Lingham

Your crazy songs you send me and your positive energy that radiates one thing, and that's a smile. Thank you for caring and maintaining a true friendship and loyalty that has been truly a blessing. I love you my dear crazy, lovely friend.

Grace Beament

My dear, darling friend. If anyone knows how painful a loss is, it's you. You have blessed me with faith within my heart. Our lengthy conversations on life after a loss was of a great help for me. The beautiful Rebecca Watts brought the unity of a family together that will be eternal as will Rebecca's legacy live on. God bless you my dearest loyal friend. I love you.

Annamarie Wenham

Friendships were born when Rebecca brought us all together and we have shared tears together and witnessed heartache together. Thank you, darling, for staying by my side and BEKS legacy will live on for eternal life. Rebecca's magical smile will bless others. I love you.

Reya Watts

Our darling, Reya. Your mother's magical smile lives within you. The magic of a legacy that will continue to radiate that magic which you bring for us all. Your smile is our energy and your lovely mum would be so very proud of you as we all are, too. We love you, Reya.

Vicky and Lorna

My heart and soul, loves you, both. You lost a little angel which I was so blessed to have known and Princess Lyrah will never leave my heart. I made a promise I would never leave your side and even though you all were battling your tragic loss, you all still showed me love of a family which I gained with you all. We are family and I will love you all eternally. God bless Princess Lyrah, our angel, somewhere over the rainbow. xxx

Poppy

My fluffy ball of real unconditional love. You have given me real love that has no motive; it's pure and real. You lie beside me when I feel low, you make me smile when I wake in the morning and you give me a purpose and a reason to care and love again. I love you, Poppy cat with all my heart and soul. My life saver. My soulmate. My world. xxx

Thank you to my beautiful friends that saved my life. You all held my hand and didn't let go.

I dedicate this book to my dear mother and father
My two angels, Rebecca Watts and Princess Lyrah
God bless your souls in heaven, until we meet again.
Someday I'll wish upon a star and wake up where the clouds are far behind me
Where troubles melt like lemon drops
That's where you'll find me.

CPSIA information can be obtained
at www.ICGtesting.com
Printed in the USA
BVHW092214301122
653184BV00009B/81